theHERO

how the story of God shapes our life together

STEVE KROEKER

The Hero: How the Story of God Shapes Our Life Together

© 2011 by Steve Kroeker

ISBN: 978-1-257-90759-5

Some names have been changed to protect identities.

To Melissa, sweeter than honey

table of contents

acknowledgements

First of all I'd like to thank the family of Tsawwassen Alliance Church. It's a privilege to labour alongside you in the service of the King. Special thanks to the staff and elders for their support, friendship and encouragement. Thank-you to Sharalee for all your tireless work on this project.

Thank-you to all those who have modelled a gospel-shaped life for me. I've learned and experienced gospel-shaped community, worship and mission from your life's example.

Thank-you to Tim Keller. We've never met, but your writing and speaking has been so valuable to my own growth in the gospel.

Thank-you to my parents and my family for your love, encouragement, prayers and support.

Thank-you to my amazing wife Melissa for your support, advice, love, partnership and wisdom. You are truly a gift and I thank God for you. To my kids, Noah, Eva and Jeremy: I love you guys and am praying that you meet the Hero and that the gospel radically shapes your life.

Thank-you to the great Author of the Story. Writing has been an act of worship. I pray that you would be glorified and the gospel would advance. May your kingdom come. Soli Deo Gloria.

welcome to the story

"I had always felt life first as a story: and if there is a story there is a story-teller."
– G.K. Chesterton

Ten billion dollars. That's how much North American movie-goers spend at the movie box office per year. We love stories. In a good story that's well told, we'll become emotionally invested in the characters and *need* to see them succeed. We need to see the hero take down the villain, rescue the damsel in distress, save the masses and receive the glory and fame he's due. Against all obstacles, the hero overcomes the odds and saves the day.

It seems we particularly love underdog stories. The protagonist is just an ordinary person, discounted or ignored by most everyone, not expected to amount to much or to make a difference. The 1993 film *Rudy*, starring Sean Astin, has become the classic underdog tale. Rudy is a small town boy who always dreamed of playing football for Notre Dame. But Rudy didn't have the size, the athleticism or the grades needed to make it, and everyone lets him know. Through hard work and sheer determination, Rudy eventually makes it to Notre Dame, makes the team and finally sees the field in the last game of his senior year, sacking the quarterback on the last play of the game. It's a heart-warming, nothing-can-stop-you, never-give-up story. And there's a million more like it. The underdog rises from obscurity, overcomes the odds, proves everyone wrong and becomes the hero that he knew himself to be. We love these stories. They give us hope that we too can spring out of nowhere. We also are a diamond in the rough waiting to be found. You and I are just a pile of determination away from accomplishing anything we want to.

But what if it's not true? What if we aren't a hero waiting to be born? I occasionally watch the show *American Idol*. Watching the final performances at the end is entertaining, but what I find the most amusing are the auditions at the beginning of the show. When I sing in public I have been known to bring people to tears... out of pain. My children often beg me to stop singing. So I have full admiration for those people who are terrible singers like me, yet are determined to audition anyways. That takes more guts than I have. But what I find so amusing are the people who are awful but will never admit it. After a painfully bad audition and being told they aren't good enough, they get furious at the judges and rant and rave about how they'll show them someday. These people genuinely believe that they are bona fide stars waiting to be discovered. "Someday those nasty talent scouts will see the truth and I'll show everyone how amazing I really am!" The rest of us watch on TV and marvel at the total lack of self-awareness. And yet, this seems to be our default setting as humans. We each believe we deserve much better than we've received.

Most of us view history as a long collection of short stories. Everyone is writing their own tale, with themselves as the hero. Right now, many obstacles may stand between us and our dreams, but someday we will overcome the challenges, prove the doubters wrong and show ourselves to be the hero that we know ourselves to be. We work to be our own saviour and to overcome our hard circumstances. We try to prove ourselves to be the hero by looking for salvation from our many problems and challenges.

Some seek salvation in being wildly successful, others in building wealth and security, others in sexual encounters and still others in gaining power and control. These are just a few ways that people work to overthrow their struggles and be the hero of their own story. We believe that sex, wealth, power and fame will save us from our monotonous life and the trouble we face and will show ourselves to be the hero we know ourselves to be.

How's this working out for us? In the last year or so we've watched the painful self-destruction of Charlie Sheen and the incredible fall from grace of Tiger Woods. These and many others, have demonstrated how money, fame, sex, success and admiration won't save you. It will never be enough. It will never bring you the meaning and significance you crave.

Recently I met with a woman who had just gotten engaged to be married. She knew that he wasn't really a good guy, she was aware that he had been divorced, and had a long history of cheating on his previous wife with multiple partners. He also struggled with alcoholism and the baggage that comes along with that. He claimed to be a Christian, but it was clear it was just something he said to please his girlfriend. She had been single for a while and had come to believe that if only she got married it would save her from the loneliness and pain of her childhood. She believed that marriage was the saviour that she needed, even a bad marriage would bring her the joy, satisfaction and significance that she craved. Looking to a spouse to save you—even the best spouse—is to look for disappointment.

WRONG HERO

We've got the story all wrong. This is why life can be so painful at times. We make saviours out of people and things that are incapable of saving us. We look to ourselves to overcome and be the hero we can never be. We spend our whole lives pursuing wealth and believing that if we get the elusive "enough", we will finally arrive and satisfy our souls, but it never comes. Some sacrifice everything and drop all their standards and hopes to get married, believing that companionship, to anyone, will heal their brokenness. Feeling unsatisfied, others will leave their marriage, believing that a new partner, a new experience or a new situation will fill their deepest cravings and save them from their pain. We could tell story after story of failed saviours and their broken promises.

Instead of seeing ourselves as the hero of our own story, we need to flip the script and understand our lives in light of God's story. History is not 10 billion short stories with 10 billion heroes, but is one meta-narrative, the one unifying story of God. God is the author of history and he invites us into *his* story. He calls us to quit our striving to be the hero of our own story, and to define ourselves by his story. True meaning, purpose and joy come as we find ourselves as minor characters in God's grand and sweeping narrative.

In God's story, there is only one Hero. Only One can save the day. Only One will overthrow evil, rescue the hurting, bring justice and peace and restore what was lost. Here's a hint: you aren't that hero. You and I aren't the ones who save the day. We are the ones who need rescuing, who need a hero to save us and restore us. In the grand meta-narrative of history, Jesus is the only true Hero. He's the Rescuer that we need.

As we work to make ourselves the hero, or as we look for salvation from our problems in wealth, fame, sex, power or a million other things, we are setting up competing heroes. We are trying to find a hero other than Jesus that will save us from our pain and brokenness. But these false saviours always, always disappoint. In the end there is one Hero. The story of God is the story of a good creation that becomes broken, sinful and rebellious, and the good news of our Hero Jesus Christ defeating evil, reconciling us to God and restoring all that has been lost.

WELCOME TO THE STORY

What are the questions you ask when you are deciding to go see a play or a movie? Don't you want to know something about the genre of the story? Who's in the starring role? What's the general plot of the story? There's obviously a big difference between the latest Hugh Grant romantic comedy and a Tom Cruise blow-up-absolutely-everything action thriller. It sure would be confusing to expect the former, while seeing the latter. In advance of a couple hours of entertainment we research and learn in order to properly understand the story were about to experience. It's so strange then, that most of us enter the drama of life without asking these basic questions. As Helmut Thielicke asks, "but does not everything depend on knowing these things?"[1]

In the first part of this book, we'll unpack the story of God. We'll look at the good beginning, all that went wrong and how sin corrupts everything. We'll examine the life of Jesus and what he accomplished through his death and resurrection. And we'll look at what God will accomplish to bring full restoration to our broken world.

In the second part, we'll look closely at what life looks like in the story of God. How does the good news of Jesus' victory shape our life now? What does life look like when we identify in God's story instead of writing our own?

I invite you into this journey and to consider the story of God.

---

[1] Helmut Thielicke, *How the World Began: Man in the First Chapters of the Bible* (Philadelphia: Fortress, 1961), 73.

PART ONE

the Story

Chapter 1

the very good beginning

"I read the news today, oh boy" – The Beatles

This morning I woke to the news of a shooting spree in Norway. A 32-year old Norwegian man, Anders Behring Breivik, dressed as a police officer, set off a bomb in Oslo and then opened fire on a group of students at a summer camp. He ended up killing 76 people.

Yesterday a friend's 7-month old baby had to have a six hour surgery to remove a kidney that was filled with cancer. Soon they'll be putting her fragile 15 lb. body through chemotherapy.

We may not personally experience the horrors of cancer or terrorism, but we each experience pain and brokenness of different kinds. With about half of marriages failing, families are left broken and wounded. One in four women and one in six men will be sexually assaulted at some point in their lifetime.[2] We witness earthquakes and tsunamis, flooding and wildfires. We watch older generations suffer as their bodies decay and shut down. Some experience the horrors of severe mental illness,

---

[2] Justin S. Holcomb and Lindsay A. Holcomb, *Rid of My Disgrace: Hope and Healing for Victims of Sexual Assault* (Wheaton, IL: Crossway Books, 2011), 31.

while we all experience pain of one degree or another.

Whatever our upbringing, cultural background or beliefs about God, we can surely all agree that this is not the way the world is supposed to be. Something's broken.

BACK TO THE START

As we seek to know and identify in God's story, we need to go back to the beginning and understand the world as God created it to be. First we need to see that God creates, and he creates with purpose and order. The very first words of the Bible are "In the beginning God created the heavens and the earth."[3] The world is not a tragic accident or a product of random chance. This world is a created world. And not only is it created, but it was created with purpose. There is order, structure and rhythm to God's creation. There is purpose, design and intentionality in all its detail.

Often Christians want to argue about how old the earth is and answer questions of science from the beginning of Genesis, but that misses the point. The ancient neighbours of the people of Israel also had creation stories. As you compare the beginning of Genesis with the ancient creation myths what stands out is how God created the world with intentionality and design. In the stories of their contemporaries the earth was one big accident. The ancient Babylonians believed that the world was created when the goddess Tiamat is killed by the god Marduk. Her dead body is split in two to make the heavens and the earth. Everyone had a creation myth and the repeated theme was creation through death and accident.

Additionally, in the stories of their neighbours, creation was viewed as evil. But in the first chapter of Genesis, the repeated refrain is that

---

[3] Genesis 1:1

"God saw that it was good". Six times we're told that God looked at what he had created and concluded that it was good.[4] And then after the creation of humankind, Genesis 1:31 summarizes, "And God saw everything that he had made, and behold, it was very good." There is no Hebrew word for perfect, linguistically, "very good" is the best that something can be. While we may look at our world and see pain, sickness, death and evil, this was not the way it was in the beginning. There was no death, no evil, no pain, no brokenness. Everything was good and glorious.

Shakespeare said "to err is human." The Bible disagrees. All humans are in error, infected with sin and prone to evil, but that's not how God created us to be. Creation is not the problem. To "err" is a distortion of creation and a violence against what it means to be truly human.

IMAGING GOD

At the pinnacle of his creation, God creates the first man and the first woman. Genesis 1:27 tells us, "So God created man in his own image, in the image of God he created him; male and female he created them." Distinct from the rest of God's good creation, humankind is created in the *image of God*. To image God is to reflect God, or to look like him in some way. Like how a mirror reflects an image, humans reflect the image of God.

This is not to say that we *are* God. Just as you would never say that your image in the mirror *is* you. You aren't *in* the mirror; an *image* of you is in the mirror. It looks like you, but isn't actually you.

My wife and I have three kids, each of whom look quite similar to each other. I can't count how many times in the first week of his life I called my youngest son, Jeremy, by his older brother's name. They

---

[4] Genesis 1:4, 10, 12, 18, 21, 25

look so similar! Our kids also look like us in many ways. They have my
chin and ears, but my wife's fair skin, light hair and blue eyes. They also
take after our personality traits and mannerisms in many ways. People
often remark how our kids look or act like one or both of us. The way
children look and act like their parents is similar to the way that humans
image or look like God. When God created humankind, he made them
to reflect him. Humans carry on the family resemblance of their Father
who made them.

Sometimes people like to get really precise and pinpoint one specific
way that we reflect God and conclude that that one thing *is* the image
of God. In reality, we image God in many ways. As humans have a
spirit, they reflect the God who is spirit. As humans live in community,
they reflect the three-in-one triune God who is a model community. As
humans exercise authority, dominion and care over creation, they reflect
the God who in his sovereignty sustains and upholds his creation. As
humans create technology, art, beauty and music, they reflect The Artist,
the God who loves creativity and beauty. As humans demonstrate love,
sacrifice and generosity, they reflect our loving, sacrificial and generous
God.

As we live more and more in godliness we reflect God more clear-
ly. Even after sin enters the world and infects us, we remain bearers
of God's image, distorted though that may be at times.[5] As Driscoll &
Breshears write, "as sinners, we remain God's mirrors, but mirrors that
have been thrown to the floor and broken and scattered into numer-
ous shards and bits. Consequently, we reflect the glory and goodness
of God infrequently and poorly."[6] Though the mirror is broken, and
reflects poorly, it still reflects God.

---

[5] See Genesis 9:6 where people remain image bearers even after the fall.
[6] Mark Driscoll and Gerry Breshears, *Doctrine: What Christians Should Believe* (Wheaton, IL: Crossway Books, 2010), 138.

INHERENT WORTH

One of the significant implications of the doctrine of being made in God's image is that all humans have inherent worth, dignity and value. Our value as humans comes not from our accomplishments and success, accumulated wealth and prosperity, or physical abilities, but from our creation in God's image. We need to derive our worth, not from our accomplishments and experiences but from how God has made each person as an image-bearer.

This point is crucial and so many people get it wrong. We tend to believe that we'll be loved and valued by God if we perform well or meet expectations. Just last week I met with a woman who didn't understand her inherent value as an image bearer. Though she wouldn't say it in these terms, she believed value was found in being married, having children and finding the approval and love of others. Being single and unable to have children she felt worthless. By misunderstanding the Story of God, she carried false beliefs about herself which distorted her outlook. To live in the story of God, we need to remember the truth about ourselves, that we are made in God's image and carry inherent value and worth.

That every human is created in the image of God is the reason why murder is so wrong. The first time in the Bible that we're told that murder is forbidden, the reason given is "for God made man in his own image."[7] Killing a person is altogether different than killing a plant or even an animal. A person is an image-bearer of God.

The story of evolution teaches the principle of survival of the fittest. The strong are right to devour or leave behind the weak if the weak are slowing them down. The interests of the species are always ahead of the interests of the weak. In this line of thinking the Nazi's murdered

---

[7] Genesis 9:6

an estimated 200,000 people with mental illness. Hitting a little closer to home, in 2005, there were 96,815 abortions reported in Canada.[8] The strong devour the weak.

But in the Story of God, the weak have inherent value as image bearers of God. Your parents may have made a mistake, but God created you with intentionality, creativity and design. He made you in his own image, built with inherent worth and dignity. You matter because you were made by God to look like God.

SHALOM

When the Old Testament describes creation as it was meant to be it uses the Hebrew word *shalom*. Cornelius Plantinga explains,

> the webbing together of God, humans, and all creation in justice, fulfillment, and delight is what the Hebrew prophets call *shalom*. We call it peace, but it means far more than mere peace of mind of a cease-fire between enemies. In the Bible, shalom means *universal flourishing, wholeness and delight* – a rich state of affairs in which natural needs are satisfied and natural gifts fruitfully employed, a state of affairs that inspires joyful wonder as its Creator and Savior opens doors and welcomes the creatures in whom he delights. Shalom, in other words, is the way things ought to be.[9]

Shalom is the way that God created thing to be. Everything flourishing. Everything in its proper rhythm. In *shalom* all work is productive work and all rest is truly restful and energizing. Each body is healthy and strong, and each soul is well nourished. Relationships are marked with

[8] According to Statistics Canada. Available at http://www.statcan.gc.ca/pub/82-223-x/82-223-x2008000-eng.pdf
[9] Cornelius Plantinga, Jr. *Not the Way It's Supposed to Be: A Breviary of Sin* (Grand Rapids, MI: Eerdmans, 1995), 10.

trust and intimacy, free from abuse and betrayal.

It's the loss of *shalom* that we mourn as our heart sinks at news footage of flooding in New Orleans or when a friend tells us she's learned she has cancer. Being created in God's image and knowing that this world is broken, our souls long for *shalom*. We see and admire the beauty and goodness of God's creation, but we also recognize the brokenness and ugliness of the world in its current state.

Living in the story of God means starting where the Bible starts with God's good creation and recognizing our identity as image-bearers of God. Whatever sin, brokenness, pain and disorder we face in life, we need to start with the premise that this world is designed with purpose and order by a God who calls us to image him to the world.

This is life as God created it to be. So, where did it all go so terribly wrong?

chapter 2

the insurmountable conflict

"Houston, we have a problem" – Jim Lovell in *Apollo 13*

So what went so terribly wrong? How did we go from *shalom* to the world as we now know it? How did we go from "universal flourishing, wholeness and delight" to the futility and brokenness we experience now?

As mentioned before, everyone is in agreement that *something* wrong with the world. Where they disagree is identifying what specifically has gone wrong. Some suggest that the problem is a lack of education and opportunities for all. There's crime and poverty only because of a lack of opportunities. If only we could provide education for all it would solve many of our problems. Others think authority and corruption is the problem and that democracy is the answer. If we were to bring democracy to the world we would eliminate power-hungry and oppressive leadership. Others still suggest that a lack of morality is the problem and the answer is moral law. As long as people are permitted to live immorally we will continue to use and abuse each other. If governments were to legislate stricter moral laws, much of our problems would be solved. Each Story has a view of what's wrong. The Bible, however, names our great problem as sin.

Genesis 3 tells us of how in paradise, the serpent comes and tempts the first woman, Eve. He questions God's word and his character, and plants seeds of doubt: "did God *actually* say...?"[10] Through the serpent's questioning, Eve begins to trust in the word of the serpent over the word of God. She places her faith in the serpent's lies over God's truth, doubting his goodness. So she disobeyed the command of God and ate the fruit she and Adam were commanded not to. Adam actively joined her in this rebellion.[11]

The apostle Paul summarized sin by stating "they exchanged the truth about God for a lie and worshiped and served the creature rather than the Creator, who is blessed forever."[12] They rejected the good word from God in favor of the lies of the creature. They worshipped the creature rather than the Creator. The heart of sin is this exchange, trading God's ideal for a shoddy imitation.

Imagine the foolishness of someone trading in a brand new Lamborghini straight up for a beat down 1983 Honda Civic with 400,000 kilometers on it and thinking that they *upgraded*. This is insane! What a horrible exchange. Why would they do that? "Well the used car salesman told us that this Civic was a much better car. The Lamborghini was really limiting us." The sad reality is that because of the lies of the universe's greasy car salesman, we traded our Lamborghini for a pile of metal and we actually believe we won the trade.

---

[10] Genesis 3:1, emphasis mine.
[11] Genesis 3:6
[12] Romans 1:25

DEFINING SIN

All sin finds its root in a false worship. We sin because we worship created things rather than the Creator. We elevate and delight in things other than God, looking for joy, purpose and meaning in created things. D.A. Carson says, "the heart of all this evil is idolatry itself. It is the de-godding of God."[13] Sin dethrones God and replaces him with something, anything else, even something otherwise good and honorable.

I was talking with a man who was seeking freedom from substance abuse in a twelve step program. He explained how he'll need to seek forgiveness from anyone he's hurt, but ultimately he'll need to learn to forgive himself. In his view—one shared by many others—in any sinful or destructive behavior, your ultimate offense is against *yourself.* You need to forgive you.

Is that right? Is sin ultimately against yourself more anyone else? Psalm 51 is a song or prayer of repentance written by King David. David had sex with Bathsheba, a married woman, gotten her pregnant and then to cover it up, he had her husband Uriah killed. Adultery. Murder. Lies. Cover-up. An ancient sex scandal.

Who had he offended? Well, certainly Uriah, he's dead. Bathsheba as well. She's pregnant with a child of a man she's not married to. What of David's family? The nation that he was called to rule over in righteousness? All that is true. We often don't see how many people are affected by our sin. Like a grenade, our destructive behavior always projects shrapnel which injures everyone near us as well. David's sin has certainly brought damage to many people, but David gets it right when he says to God, "Against you, you only, have I sinned and done what is evil in your sight."[14] We don't sin against ourselves, we sin against God.

When we sin, we dethrone God, reject his righteous rule and place

---

[13] D.A. Carson, *Christ and Culture Revisited* (Grand Rapids, MI: Eerdmans, 2008), 5.
[14] Psalm 51:4

something else on his throne in his place. We don't sin against ourselves, because it wasn't our throne. Our behavior is sinful because we've de-godded God. When we sin, God is always the most offended party.[15]

Sin is also a false belief. We exchange the truth for a lie, swapping out reality for a wrong belief about reality. We start to doubt God's promises and his goodness and we place our trust in distortions. Instead of receiving God's word as truth, we question: "did God *really* say...?" We are constantly being given two—or more, I suppose—competing promises. Both God and Satan preach a sermon to us. They both present a picture of reality, a worldview. Our behavior reflects which promise we believe. When we sin, we are rejecting the truth of God, doubting that his word and promise are really true, and we are placing our faith and trust in the lies and false promises of sin.

For Eve (and Adam), they had been given two competing messages. From God they had been given a creation that was good, vibrant and flourishing. We're told that "out of the ground the LORD God made to spring up every tree that is pleasant to the sight and good for food."[16] God had generously created a good and flourishing world for them to enjoy. However, God had warned them that to eat of the tree of the knowledge of good and evil would lead to their death. But the serpent came along and preached an altogether different sermon. He questioned God's goodness and truthfulness. God is afraid of you. He doesn't want you to become like he is. You can't trust God, he's holding good things back from you. Presented with these two conflicting messages, Eve and Adam chose to believe the word of the serpent and to disbelieve the word of God. All sin follows this pattern: disbelief in God's good word and a belief in the lies and false promises of Satan. We sin because we

---

[15] We may need to forgive ourselves as well, we may have caused great damage to ourselves, but sin is ultimately always against God.
[16] Genesis 2:9

fail to believe.

Plantinga defines sin as "culpable *shalom*-breaking."[17] He explains,

Sin is not only the breaking of law but also the breaking of covenant with one's savior. Sin is the smearing of a relationship, the grieving of one's divine parent and benefactor, a betrayal of the partner to whom one is joined by a holy bond…. All sin has first and finally a Godward force. Sin is a culpable and personal affront to a personal God.[18]

This is why God hates sin. He has to. Sin is not just the breaking of law, but is a violation of *shalom*, it's war on the way the world was supposed to be.

A father who is apathetic and disinterested when his daughter is attacked and violated would be almost as evil as the perpetrator who committed this crime. A good father is rightfully angry at violence towards his loved ones. Likewise God, being holy, is rightfully upset when his beautiful and good creation is being violated and attacked over and over again. Anything less would be evil.

Often people associate sin with wrongs things that we *do*, thinking of sin as active rule-breaking. The biblical story won't allow for such a narrow definition. Jesus taught, "You have heard that it was said, 'You shall not commit adultery.' But I say to you that everyone who looks at a woman with lustful intent has already committed adultery with her in his heart."[19] All adultery is sin, whether it happens in the privacy of your mind or in the privacy of a Best Western while on a business trip. Certainly murdering your boss is sinful, but so is having murderous desire and hatred restrained only by the threat of consequences. That's not an

---

[17] Plantinga, Jr. *Not the Way It's Supposed to Be,* 14.
[18] Ibid., 12-13.
[19] Matthew 5:27-28

honourable restraint, but a selfish one, displaying even further sinful attitudes.

You don't kill your boss because of superior ethics but because you selfishly want to avoid the consequences of killing. It's easier to endure your boss. You'd rather put up with him than be free of your boss and be in prison. Our restrained behaviour is more often motivated by fear of consequences than by pure desires and good will towards others.

Additionally, we can sin through *inaction*. James 4:17 says, "So whoever knows the right thing to do and fails to do it, for him it is sin." We can sin through choosing to do nothing when something should be done. Invading Poland is evil. And so is standing by and doing nothing when something could be done.

DEATH AND ALL HIS FRIENDS

The consequences of sin are many. We see these consequences emerge immediately once Adam and Eve sin against God. They first experience shame and guilt for their disobedience and pathetically try to cover their shame. Their relationship with God is now broken and fractured. They run from God in fear and hide from him. When questioned about their disobedience, Adam passes the blame on to Eve, who passes the blame on to the serpent. Instead of accepting responsibility, they turn on each other, make excuses and shift blame. Because of their sin, the whole of creation experiences a cursed and futile existence. Life is futile and painful. Adam will fight with the weeds in futility all the rest of his days. Finally, death was introduced as a consequence of sin. Adam is told that he'll work the ground until he joins the ground.

These same consequences are what make life so difficult today. Because of our sin we experience separation from God. We've made God our enemy and live in rebellion and treason against the creator God of the universe. We've each removed God from his rightful throne and sat down in his chair, claiming his glory and divine rights. Having made God our enemy, we don't experience intimacy and covenant with God. We don't delight in God and find satisfaction in his presence.

That conflict also extends to our relationships with each other. Like our first parents, we pass blame, avoid responsibility for wrong and make excuses. The pain and difficulty in dating and marriage has given stand-up comedians an endless supply of material as we suffer the anxiety and pain of conflict-soaked relationships. Think about that: even in marriage, the most beautiful and intimate relationship of trust and love, we experience much conflict and pain. Even our best relationships are difficult. Our sinful disposition leads us to lie and cheat on each other, to use and abuse, and to seek our own good instead of others. We are proud, selfish and combative creatures, quick to defend, quick to attack, quick to cause pain. Sin has introduced violence, pain and conflict in *all* our relationships.

Sin also brings guilt for the wrong that we have committed. I don't just mean that we *feel* guilty, but that we actually *are* guilty, even if we don't feel it. Because of our sin we stand under the justice of God for our wrong. This isn't God being harsh or unfair. It's the simple fact that we've done wrong and we've been caught red-handed. We stand guilty.

Likewise we suffer shame for both the sin committed by us, as well as the sin that's been committed against us. To deal with our shame we lie, cover up and make excuses. A politician caught in a sex scandal will tell bold-face lies until the evidence is insurmountable, at which point he'll go into damage control, apology and spin mode. Instead of confession and repentance, we act like our first parents, pathetically attempting to cover our shame with fig leaves. We hide our sin, utilizing denial, spin, blame-shifting and false repentance as tools for covering ourselves.

We're so skilled at deceiving others and covering our sin, that we're even able to cover our shame with religion. We mask our evil with respectability and good deeds. We work to compensate our sin with church attendance or serving others. The fig leaf of charity temporarily assuages our guilt and eases our conscience, but in the end it does not actually deal with our shame or sin. Like our first parents, we continue to find new and creative ways to cover our shame and avoid responsibility for our sin.

Finally, sin has introduced death into the world. Without sin there would be no cancer, no decaying bodies, no tragic death. When I first became a pastor, a family in our church buried two baby boys in under three years. Imagine the pain and heartache. Imagine owning a big farm house and only wanting to fill it with a large family and then comes death. There is something so horribly wrong about little caskets. Those little black boxes scream "this is all wrong!" Children should never be buried by their parents, never mind their grandparents! Whether 8 hours old or 80 years old, we know there is always something wrong about death. The Apostle Paul wrote that "the wages of sin is death."[20] Death is the just payment for the sin we have committed. What's frightening is that for those outside the grace of God, there awaits a second death, an eternal separation from God.[21]

BORN THIS WAY

Sin, like a genetic disease, has been passed down to us from our first parents. It has corrupted and infected us so that we have this natural bent towards sin. We are all sinners both by nature and by subsequent choice.

Author and blogger Fred Sanders recently noted that there's been a

---

[20] Romans 6:23; also Romans 5:12; 7:13; James 1:15
[21] Revelation 2:11; 20:6, 14; 21:8

recent theme in pop songs to promote relentless self-affirmation.[22] Katy Perry sings:

> there's a spark in you
> you just gotta ignite the light
> and let it shine...
> Cause baby you're a firework
> come on show'em what you're worth.

In her chart-topping song "Born this Way", Lady Gaga sings:

> I'm beautiful in my way
> 'Cause God makes no mistakes
> I'm on the right track baby
> I was born this way
> Don't hide yourself in regret
> Just love yourself and you're set
> I'm on the right track baby
> I was born this way

Let's just ignore the beautiful irony of someone with a well-planned and well-marketed persona, including a stage name and costumes, singing about being born this way. The message of these songs (and many more like them) is that you were born awesome, so just be true to yourself, even if you are a misfit, no—especially if you are a misfit. Don't let anyone question your innate awesomeness. Just be you, because you're awesome!

So far, in the story of God, we've seen that we aren't born awesome, but broken. We aren't a firework ready to show off our awesomeness, but a broken image-bearer needing to be restored. We have tremendous

---

[22] http://www.scriptoriumdaily.com/2011/02/17/born-this-way-so-raise-your-glass-all-you-fireworks/

value, yes, but that value comes from how we are created to reflect God, not from an innate awesomeness that deserves worship. We aren't "on the right track", but are born on the wrong track, in rebellion against God, violating *shalom* and helpless to change.

A GLIMPSE OF HOPE

Does this all feel a little depressing? It may, but by God's grace this is not the end of the story. Even as Adam and Eve are experiencing the effects of sin and being driven out of paradise, there is a glimpse of hope for them. We're told that "the Lord God made for Adam and for his wife garments of skins and clothed them."[23] Instead of leaving them to their pitiful attempts at covering their shame with fig leaves, God has mercy and provides an adequate covering for their shame. It's significant that he covers their shame with clothing made from animal skins. Here we see a foreshadowing that the shedding of blood will be required to adequately cover our shame. We need a sacrifice.

Even earlier, hope is given when God tells the serpent, "I will put enmity between you and the woman, and between your offspring and her offspring; he shall bruise your head and you shall bruise his heel."[24] God promises that this brokenness is not the way it will always be. Evil will not always win. Though the descendents of Eve will be locked in this perpetual struggle against evil, there will be a day when the offspring (singular) of Eve will bruise the head of the serpent. Hope is given that a descendent of Eve will overthrow the serpent and restore humanity back to the garden.

Someday, there will be a hero.

---

[23] Genesis 3:21
[24] Genesis 3:15

chapter 3

the hero emerges

"He became what we are that he might make us what he is" - Athanasius

Life outside the garden is hard. Adam and Eve's second child is murdered by their first child. That was not at all what she was expecting. Coming on the heels of the hope given that someday her offspring would crush the serpent, when Eve conceived and gave birth she was probably expecting Jesus but ended up with Cain. Sin spreads and life goes from bad to worse.

And yet, God in his mercy, pursues his people, working to restore them back to himself. The book of Exodus tells how God saved his people out of slavery in the land of Egypt when they were a group of nobodies. He redeemed them and gave them freedom by bringing their Egyptian oppressors to their knees. He entered into covenant with them, and showed them grace instead of judgment. He gave them his law so they would know how to live together and how to worship him. They were to be a unique people set aside as God's people, living God's way. A nation pursuing *shalom*.

But continually they would disobey, rebel against God and run to other man-made gods. They continued to exchange the truth about God for a lie and worship and serve created things rather than the Creator. And still, God showed patience and mercy to them and would save them again and again, bringing them to a place of repentance and restoration. But their new obedience would only last for a season before they would run to their idols again.

Throughout the Old Testament we see that law isn't the answer. It wasn't enough to *know* the law. Knowledge wasn't the problem. They didn't need more rules or behavior modification, they needed new hearts. Infected by sin, they loved worshipping themselves more than worshipping God. They loved seeking for themselves, rather than seeking after God. Their behavior was an outflow of their broken hearts. That's not to say that the Law was bad, it wasn't. But the Law doesn't fix the problem of hearts infected with sin.

But this is not the end of the story. Scattered throughout the Old Testament are promises of a new covenant, a time when God would do a new work. God promised through the prophet Jeremiah,

> Behold, the days are coming, declares the LORD, when I will make a new covenant with the house of Israel and the house of Judah... I will put my law within them, and I will write it on their hearts. And I will be their God, and they shall be my people. And no longer shall each one teach his neighbor and each his brother, saying, 'Know the LORD,' for they shall all know me, from the least of them to the greatest, declares the LORD. For I will forgive their iniquity, and I will remember their sin no more.[25]

The Prophet Isaiah adds,

> I will sprinkle clean water on you, and you shall be clean from

---

[25] Jeremiah 31:31, 33-34

all your uncleannesses, and from all your idols I will cleanse you. And I will give you a new heart, and a new spirit I will put within you. And I will remove the heart of stone from your flesh and give you a heart of flesh. And I will put my Spirit within you, and cause you to walk in my statutes and be careful to obey my rules.[26]

Jeremiah pictures a new day when God would write his law right on their hearts and they would not fail to be his people. With new hearts they would no longer desire and pursue rebellion, but would finally be able to obey God and live in *shalom*. God's very own Spirit would dwell within them and empower them to live in righteousness.

There would be no need to teach each other about God, because *everyone* would already know him. Tim Keller summarizes the prophets message, saying "someday the glory of God would cover the earth as the waters fill the sea—in other words, the whole world would become a holy of holies. The whole earth would be filled with the glory and presence of God again."[27] Their sin and rebellion will be forgiven and forgotten forever.

How would this new covenant happen? How would God bring about this new restoration with new hearts and new obedience? God promises not a new law, but a saviour king who will redeem his people, forgive sin, overthrow death and restore *shalom*. The prophet Isaiah writes,

> For to us a child is born,
>
>   to us a son is given;
>
> and the government shall be upon his shoulder,
>
>   and his name shall be called
>
> Wonderful Counselor, Mighty God,
>
>   Everlasting Father, Prince of Peace.

---

[26] Ezekiel 36:25-27

[27] Timothy Keller, *King's Cross: The Story of the World in the Life of Jesus* (New York: Dutton, 2011), 158-9.

Of the increase of his government and of peace
   there will be no end,
on the throne of David and over his kingdom,
   to establish it and to uphold it
with justice and with righteousness
   from this time forth and forevermore.[28]

God promised a child, a Son, who would be none less than the "Mighty God" and "Everlasting Father". This God-Man would be a king of justice and righteousness, who would bring a kingdom of peace.

Later, Isaiah describes a figure he calls "The Servant of the LORD" who sacrifices himself for the people. Describing the Servant he says,

Surely he has borne our griefs
   and carried our sorrows;
yet we esteemed him stricken,
   smitten by God, and afflicted.
But he was wounded for our transgressions;
   he was crushed for our iniquities;
upon him was the chastisement that brought us peace,
   and with his stripes we are healed.
All we like sheep have gone astray;
   we have turned—every one—to his own way;
and the LORD has laid on him
   the iniquity of us all....
he poured out his soul to death
   and was numbered with the transgressors;
yet he bore the sin of many,
   and makes intercession for the transgressors.[29]

---

[28] Isaiah 9:6-7
[29] Isaiah 53:4-6, 12

God graciously foretells of how the sin (iniquity, transgression) of
the people would be covered through the sacrificial death of the Servant. This one man would bring life to many though his death in their
place.

The entire Old Testament is pointing ahead towards the Hero who
will redeem all that was lost when sin entered the world. The Old Testament shows us that we don't need a law to save us, we need a Saviour. The entire Old Testament is pointing ahead to Jesus, its 39 books
are like a musical score that build and builds in anticipation but never
reaches the note that will resolve it all. The Old Testament is a book
of promises made and of hope given. Without the New Testament,
the Old Testament is deeply unsatisfying, and with it everything makes
sense and finds its fullness.

JESUS' BIRTH

As prophesied in the Scriptures, Jesus was miraculously born of a vir-
gin[30] in the town of Bethlehem.[31] When the angel appeared to Jesus'
mother Mary to announce that all this would happen, he said

> You will conceive in your womb and bear a son, and you shall call
> his name Jesus. He will be great and will be called the Son of the
> Most High. And the Lord God will give to him the throne of his
> father David, and he will reign over the house of Jacob forever,
> and of his kingdom there will be no end.[32]

And then he tells her "the child to be born will be called holy—
the Son of God."[33] On the night of Jesus' birth, angels appeared to

---

[30] Isaiah 7:14
[31] Micah 5:2
[32] Luke 1:31-33
[33] Luke 1:35

shepherds in the area announcing "unto you is born this day in the city of David a Savior, who is Christ the Lord."[34] Upon meeting the eight day old baby Jesus, a man named Simeon prophesied, "for my eyes have seen your salvation that you have prepared in the presence of all peoples."[35] At Jesus' birth, witness after witness testifies that this miraculous child is the One whom God had promised. He is the righteous King, the promised Rescuer and Redeemer, the One to save humanity and restore *shalom*.

JESUS' REMARKABLE LIFE

Jesus was raised by his mother Mary and his adopted father, Joseph who was a carpenter and a righteous man. Jesus had at least four brothers and two sisters.[36] He grew up in a fairly ordinary home, becoming a carpenter like his dad. Once his dad died, Jesus was the main breadwinner for the family. Being a carpenter he would have been a manly man with calloused hands and a strong work ethic.

Around the age of thirty he began his public ministry as an itinerant preacher. Mark writes, "after John was arrested, Jesus came into Galilee, proclaiming the gospel of God, and saying, 'The time is fulfilled, and the kingdom of God is at hand; repent and believe in the gospel.'"[37] At the core of his teaching was a proclamation of the good news (gospel) that the kingdom of God had now arrived. Jesus said "I must preach the good news of the kingdom of God to the other towns as well; for I was sent for this purpose."[38] He was sent by the Father to proclaim the arrival of the kingdom of God, that God was overthrowing sin and evil

---

[34] Luke 2:11
[35] Luke 2:30-31
[36] Matthew 13:55-56
[37] Mark 1:14-15
[38] Luke 4:43

in the life, teaching, death and resurrection of Jesus.

His teaching was accompanied by many miracles. In fulfillment of prophecy, Jesus healed the sick, gave sight to the blind, and raised the dead. These miracles confirmed Jesus' identity as the very Son of God. They also showed how the damage done through the dominance of sin in the world was becoming undone through Jesus Christ. His life was the beginning of the restoration of what was lost at the Fall of humankind.

Jesus also lived a life of perfect righteousness. While in paradise, the first man and the first woman trusted the lies of the serpent over the word of God, rejecting God and losing paradise. Jesus, out in the desert, trusted the word of God over the lies of the serpent, stayed faithful to God and earned paradise through his perfect righteousness. Jesus won victory where Adam failed.

Even the most upright and moral religious leaders like Gandhi and Mother Teresa have admitted that they are sinners, but Jesus claimed to be without sin saying, "I always do the things that are pleasing to [the Father]" and "which of you convicts me of sin? I tell the truth, why do you not believe me?"[39] This claim to be sinless was affirmed and taught by those who followed him and knew him best. Peter called him the "Holy and Righteous One"[40] and said that "He committed no sin, neither was deceit found in his mouth."[41] John said "You know that he [came] to take away sins, and in him there is no sin."[42] Even ancient, non-Christian sources claim that Jesus lived a very remarkable life. The first century Jewish historian Josephus wrote,

> Now there was about this time Jesus, a wise man, if it be lawful to call him a man; for he was a doer of wonderful works, a teacher of such men as receive the truth with pleasure. He drew over to

[39] John 8:29, 46
[40] Acts 3:14
[41] I Peter 2:22; Also see I Peter 1:19; 3:18
[42] I John 3:5

him both many of the Jews and many of the Gentiles. He was Christ. And when Pilate, at the suggestion of the principal men amongst us, had condemned him to the cross, those that loved him at the first did not forsake him; for he appeared to them alive again the third day; as the divine prophets had foretold these and ten thousand other wonderful things concerning him. And the tribe of Christians, so named from him, are not extinct to this day.[43]

As remarkable as his sinless life is, still more remarkable is the Bible's claim that Jesus is God. Jesus himself said "I and the Father are one", to which his hearers immediately picked up stones to kill him saying, "It is not for a good work that we are going to stone you but for blasphemy, because you, being a man, make yourself God."[44] On many other occasions, Jesus' words plainly revealed to his hearers that he was claiming to be God descended from heaven.[45] Additionally, the New Testament writers are unanimous in claiming that Jesus was God incarnate. John, referring to Jesus as the Word, starts his biography of Jesus by saying, "In the beginning was the Word, and the Word was with God, and the Word was God" and then adds "And the Word became flesh and dwelt among us, and we have seen his glory, glory as of the only Son from the Father, full of grace and truth."[46] The Apostle Paul calls Jesus "the image of the invisible God"[47], "our great God and Savior"[48] and "the Christ who is God over all, blessed forever."[49] Peter called him "the

[43] Flavius Josephus, *The Jewish Antiquities,* (New York: Holt, Rinheart and Winston), 18:3:3.
[44] John 10:30-33
[45] Matthew 26:63-64; Luke 5:20-21; John 6:38; 8:58-59; 17:5, 24
[46] John 1:1, 14
[47] Colossians 1:15
[48] Titus 2:13
[49] Romans 9:5

Author of Life"[50] and "our God and Savior Jesus Christ."[51] The unanimous testimony of the New Testament is that Jesus is God himself in the flesh dwelling amongst us.

JESUS' DEATH AND RESURRECTION

Even though Jesus lived without sin, performed countless miracles and was continually followed by large crowds, he was not loved by everyone. Religious leaders of different stripes were threatened by his popularity, offended by his message of radical grace, and insulted when he exposed their hypocrisy and sin. These different religious groups became united in their opposition of Jesus. When Jesus was in Jerusalem for the Passover, he was betrayed by his own disciple Judas, arrested by temple guards, tried by the High Priest, mocked and beaten, then handed over to Roman authorities to be killed. Pilate, the Roman prefect of Judea found no fault with him, but an angry mob demanded his death. Eventually Pilate gave in and ordered for Jesus to be crucified.

Jesus was then led to a place of execution outside of Jerusalem called "the Skull", where they crucified him along with two criminals. Roman crucifixion involved attaching a criminal's hands and feet to a cross, stretched out in such a way that they would slowly and painfully suffocate to death, sometimes after days of suffering. A crucifixion would happen in a public place, often outside a city or along main travel route for all those entering the city to see. By this the criminal would be publically shamed and their death would deter further rebellion. It was such a horrendous form of execution that it was reserved for the very worst of criminals and was never performed on women or roman citizens. Jesus was so badly beaten that he only survived six hours on the cross before

---

[50] Acts 3:15
[51] 2 Peter 1:1

being pronounced dead by the professional roman executioners.

With the Sabbath approaching, Jesus' body was taken down and buried in a tomb carved out of rock. To be certain that no one would steal his body, Pilate and the religious authorities sealed the tomb with a large stone and placed guards to protect it.

But at dawn on the third day (Sunday), Jesus rose from death. When some women came to the tomb early that morning, the stone had been rolled away and Jesus' body was missing. An angel appeared to them proclaiming that Jesus had risen. While on their way to tell the others Jesus appeared to the women alive and resurrected. Over the next forty days, Jesus appeared to Peter and the rest of the disciples many times, and to many, many others, including 500 at one time.[52] He also appeared to his half-brother James,[53] who had previously thought that Jesus was crazy,[54] but upon seeing him resurrected believed him to be the messiah and became a leader in the church in Jerusalem. After those forty days of teaching, Jesus ascended back to heaven, promising that he would send the Holy Spirit to empower them to take the gospel throughout the world and that someday he would return to fulfill the kingdom of God.

WHAT DO YOU DO WITH JESUS?

After reflecting on the remarkable life of Jesus Christ, what do you make of him? Was he a great prophet? A good moral teacher? An inspirational leader? God's promised redeemer? C.S. Lewis famously outlines the foolishness of minimizing Jesus simply as a good, moral teacher:

> A man who was merely a man and said the sort of things Jesus said would not be a great moral teacher. He would either be a lunatic—on

---

[52] I Corinthians 15:5-8
[53] I Corinthians 15:7
[54] Mark 3:20-21; John 7:5

a level with the man who says he is a poached egg–or else he would be the Devil of Hell. You must make your choice. Either this man was, and is, the Son of God: or else a madman or something worse. You can shut Him up for a fool, you can spit at Him and kill Him as a demon; or you can fall at His feet and call Him Lord and God. But let us not come with any patronising nonsense about His being a great human teacher. He has not left that open to us. He did not intend to.[55]

[55] C.S. Lewis, *Mere Christianity,* (New York, NY: Harper Collins, 2001), 52.

Chapter 4
the climactic victory

"Were I asked to focus the New Testament message in three words, my proposal would be adoption through propitiation, and I do not expect ever to meet a richer or more pregnant summary of the gospel than that." – J.I. Packer

In Bruno Mars' hit song "Grenade" he sings,

> I'd catch a grenade for you
> Throw my hand on a blade for you
> I'd jump in front of a train for you
> You know I'd do anything for you
> I would go through all this pain
> Take a bullet straight through my brain
> Yes, I would die for you baby

The song reveals what we all know: true and deep love is demonstrated through sacrifice. Great personal sacrifice reveals the depth of one's love. Bruno's willingness to take a bullet for his "baby" demonstrates that he values her wellbeing more than his own life, and would be willing to substitute himself in her place if she were faced with death. I have no idea if Bruno Mars actually would follow through with his bold claims, but I do know that he has hit on the truth that love is measured in sacrifice.

TRAGEDY OR GIFT?

At first you might think that Jesus' death is the sad and tragic story of an innocent sufferer, wrongly killed for crimes he did not commit. You'd be right to say that he was innocent and that his death was the ultimate injustice. However, beyond the unjust actions of wicked people, God had a design and plan all along. In fact, in the Bible we learn that God had a plan, from before creation, to exalt the glory of his grace through the death of his son.[56] His disciples may have been shocked at how these events unfolded, but Jesus had foretold his betrayal, death and resurrection many times.[57] After Jesus' ascension, Peter proclaimed that Jesus was "delivered up according to the definite plan and foreknowledge of God" and that the evil actions of Herod, Pilate and the others responsible for Jesus' death did "whatever your hand and your plan had predestined to take place."[58] The murder of Jesus was a serious sin. In fact, it was the greatest evil ever committed. Jesus was the only truly innocent sufferer. And yet, at the same time, his death was part of the eternal and good plan of God. Jesus' death was not a tragic accident as much as a loving self-sacrifice. He was not a suffering victim as much as a generous giver.

The cross is at the very heart of Christian faith. But what exactly

---

[56] Ephesians 1:3-6; Revelation 13:8; For more see John Piper, *The Pleasures of God: Meditations on God's Delight in Being God* (Sisters, OR: Multnomah Books, 2000).
[57] Matthew 12:40; 16:21; 17:22-23; 20:17-19; 21:33-44; 26:20-25; Mark 8:31-32; 9:30-32; 10:32-34; Luke 9:21-22; 43-45; 51-53; 13:31-34; 14:27; 18:31-33; 19:9-18; 22:21-22; John 13:18-30; 16:16-33
[58] Acts 2:23; 4:28

did Jesus accomplish by dying on the cross? How was his shameful and horrible death a victory and not a defeat? The Bible describes dozens of things that Jesus accomplished through his death,[59] but below we'll focus on seven of the most significant.

JESUS IS OUR REDEMPTION

We often think of sin simply as wrong things that we do. That's partly correct, but more than simply wrongful acts, sin is a force that holds people captive as slaves. The apostle Paul says, "Do you not know that if you present yourselves to anyone as obedient slaves, you are slaves of the one whom you obey, either of sin, which leads to death, or of obedience, which leads to righteousness?"[60] In that chapter he talks about sin as having dominion over people. Sin is a powerful force that enslaves and traps and ensnares people.

Sin gives us the illusion of freedom: we are free to choose right or wrong and we freely choose wrong. But while we feel that we are free, we are not. We are enslaved to sin and are unable to change and break free from its dominion.

I'm reminded of the old Bob Newhart MadTV sketch where the client shares her problems and behaviors with the therapist who instead of listening and giving advice, simply keeps yelling at the client to "STOP IT! Cut it out!" Simply willing ourselves to stop our sinful behavior will not work as long as we are enslaved to sin. What we need is not more willpower, but to be released from the power of sin. We need freedom.

The good news of the gospel is that Jesus is our redemption. On the cross Jesus purchases our freedom from the bondage of sin.[61] He

---

[59] See John Piper, *50 Reasons Why Jesus Came to Die* (Wheaton, IL: Crossway Books, 2006).
[60] Romans 6:16
[61] Titus 2.13-14

redeems enslaved sinners and sets them free. Paul says, "we know that
your old self was crucified with [Christ] in order that the body of sin
might be brought to nothing, so that we would no longer be enslaved to
sin... you have been set free from sin and have become slaves of God."[62]
Because of Christ, our master has changed. We are no longer enslaved
to sin, our old abusive master but have been set free to be obedient to
our new master. Jesus brings freedom.

JESUS IS OUR EXAMPLE

The Bible tells us that the sufferings of Jesus were given to us as an example of how to suffer well: "Christ also suffered for you, leaving you
an example, so that you might follow in his steps."[63] Theologians calls
this *Christus Exemplar*, or Christ our example. As we face hardship, suffering, pain, persecution and injustice, we should look to Jesus who was
the truly righteous sufferer. Though he was without sin and had committed no crime, he was betrayed by a close friend, arrested and tried in
a kangaroo court. He was mocked, spat on, beaten, ridiculed and reviled.
He was abandoned and denied by his closest friends and left alone in his
time of greatest need. Finally he was executed on a roman cross.

As Jesus suffered these horrendous things, there was no retaliation,
no bitterness, no anger or revenge, no deceit or sin at all. He did not
allow his hardship and suffering to lead him into a sinful response. Instead, he "continued entrusting himself to him who judges justly."[64] As
he suffered, he did not look to revenge to even the score, but he looked
to God who is the Just Judge who will render all things right in the end.
He was able to suffer well by trusting that God the Father would do his

---

[62] Romans 6:6,22
[63] I Peter 2:21
[64] I Peter 2:23

job and his perfect justice would win out in the end.

In his suffering Jesus is our example. Instead of seeking personal vengeance, Jesus was motivated by love for sinners and obedience to the Father. In his suffering, he sought to glorify the Father, by obeying his plan and rescuing a people for his own possession. Like Jesus we can endure hardship to display the glory of God to the watching world, so that all can see His worth. Like Jesus we don't have to get revenge or retaliate, but continue to trust that the Just Judge will do what is right in the end and that His sovereign plan is good, even when we don't understand it.

JESUS MAKES US CLEAN

The Bible also shows us that sin is a power that defiles us. It makes us unclean and filthy. This was a big theme of the Book of Leviticus: sin defiles and makes you unclean. Commonly, as people commit sin in private, particularly sexual sins, they feel the filth and uncleanness of their sin. They feel dirty. The overwhelming feeling is one of being stained, filthy and impure.

We also need to recognize that we are defiled not only by the sins we commit, but also by those committed against us. Victims of rape, sexual assault and other forms of abuse may be innocent victims, but the sin committed against them has defiled them and made them dirty.[65] The horrible sin has left a stain.

One of the many glories of the cross is that Jesus is our *expiation*, that is, his sacrifice removed our sin from us and made us clean. John writes

> If we walk in the light, as he is in the light, we have fellowship with one another, and the blood of Jesus his Son cleanses us from all sin.

---

[65] See Mark Driscoll and Gerry Breshears, *Death by Love: Letters From the Cross* (Wheaton, IL: Crossway, 2008), 143-160.

If we say we have no sin, we deceive ourselves, and the truth is not in us. If we confess our sins, he is faithful and just to forgive us our sins and to cleanse us from all unrighteousness.[66]

Sin defiles and makes us dirty, but Jesus makes us clean. As we confess our sin and bring it into the light, Jesus cleanses us from all sin and unrighteousness, whether evil we have committed ourselves or evil committed against us. All unrighteousness is removed from us. All is cleansed and made new again.

Our sin is not merely cancelled out and forgiven (amazing as that is), while we continue on in our filth. No, Jesus not only forgives, but makes us clean and new. We are pure, whole and beautiful again.

Our tendency is to define ourselves by the sins we've committed or have been committed against us. We build our identity on our failures and how we've been victimized. But for those who confess their sin and turn to Jesus, there is a new identity. We are no longer defined by our failure and the stains of sin, but are defined by Jesus' success and his cleansing. Because of Jesus, you can be new, clean, pure and whole, without stain, wrinkle or blemish. Because of Jesus you are beautiful.

JESUS WINS US VICTORY

Life is a battle. Whether they recognize it or not, every human is involved in a cosmic spiritual battle. It's not a physical battle waged with weapons and physical might. Paul says, "For we do not wrestle against flesh and blood, but against the rulers, against the authorities, against the cosmic powers over this present darkness, against the spiritual forces of evil in the heavenly places."[67] We're engaged in a war with real

---

[66] I John 1:7-9
[67] Ephesians 6:12

spiritual forces and cosmic powers that work for evil.

We are also in a battle against sin. We have to actively fight our sin-loving natural self. On our own, we are doomed to lose this fight. We are born in bondage to sin and stuck in our ways. We cannot change. We cannot fight. We cannot win. We try, but lose continually. We need someone to fight for us. We need a victor.

The Bible teaches that on the cross Jesus won victory for us over sin and the powers of evil. Those enemies that hurt us and had dominion over us, have been disarmed, put to shame and triumphed over. Paul says that at the cross, God "disarmed the rulers and authorities and put them to open shame, by triumphing over them in him [Jesus]."[68] Jesus defeated our enemies for us, conquering Satan, sin and death and earning the victory we could never earn for ourselves, winning the fight that we were certain to lose and lose badly.

Because of Jesus' victory on the cross, those who are in Christ can live in victory over evil powers. Demonic forces will have no power over you. They are defeated. As well, because of the victory of Christ we can—by the power of the Spirit—live in victory over our sin. We can experience victory where previously we only knew failure.

Paul tells us that now Jesus is seated at the right hand of God "far above all rule and authority and power and dominion, and above every name that is named, not only in this age but also in the one to come."[69] Jesus is the victor who reigns in power and authority over all powers and all authorities, whether physical or spiritual, past, present or future. What is there to fear when we're on Team Jesus? What power or authority can harm us when victory is won?

As Christians, we can know and live in victory, not because *we* are victorious, mighty, strong and powerful, but because Jesus won victory

---

[68] Colossians 2:15
[69] Ephesians 1:21

for us by disarming all rulers and powers on the cross. At the moment when he seemed defeated, he had truly won us eternal victory.

JESUS IS OUR RECONCILIATION

Sin also causes division and conflict both between ourselves and God and with each other. When sin entered the world, so did relational conflict. Marriage became hard and humankind was separated from God because of their sin. To this day we experience conflict, pain and heartache in our relationships. We quickly become angry and bitter towards others, responding to hurt by hurting others.

But at the cross Jesus is our reconciliation. At the cross Jesus is healing our broken relationships, both with God and each other. Paul says, "while we were enemies we were reconciled to God by the death of his Son."[70] Jesus' death heals our relationship and reconciles us back to God. His death covers the debts incurred by our conflict, heals the wounds we've created and is the agent of God's forgiveness. All hopes and attempts at reconciling with God apart from the cross are doomed for failure.

We may work to be at peace with God, but we are born his enemy thanks to the rebellion of our first parents. All our efforts at peace backfire as our hearts are prone to conflict and rebellion. We simply are unable to reconcile with God. We need him to reconcile with us, and the cross is the only means by which this is possible. He changes us from enemies to friends, from foreigners to citizens, from abandoned orphans to adopted children. God is a god of reconciliation and he accomplishes it through the cross of Christ.

Not only does Jesus death on the cross bring reconciliation to our

---

[70] Romans 5:10

hostile relationship with God, but it sets the precedent and empowers our reconciled relationships with each other. Paul writes, "Let all bitterness and wrath and anger and clamor and slander be put away from you, along with all malice. Be kind to one another, tenderhearted, forgiving one another, as God in Christ forgave you."[71] The cross becomes the example, motive and power for us to live reconciled lives in community with each other. As Christ forgives us, so to we forgive others. Instead of responding to conflict with anger and bitterness, we're called to the Christ-like response of kindness and tenderness. There is hope for healing and restoration in our broken relationships as we look to Christ our reconciliation.

JESUS SECURES OUR ADOPTION

Many people assume that God owes us kindness. He *has to* be gracious to us. The perception is that God is a generous old man, a kind grandfatherly type figure. But sin has so separated us from God that we are not family with God, we're called "aliens and strangers." We don't belong in God's home or under his roof. We're not family, he doesn't owe us anything. We're born as strangers with God, without the bond of friendship or family.

But, because of the bloody cross of Jesus, the Bible tells us "you are no longer strangers and aliens, but you are fellow citizens with the saints and members of the household of God."[72] We were foreigners, but now we're citizens. We were strangers and now we live in God's house. But we're not just guests in God's house. Paul says, "when the fullness of time had come, God sent forth his Son, born of woman, born under the law, to redeem those who were under the law, so that we might receive

---

[71] Ephesians 4:31-32
[72] Ephesians 2:19

adoption as sons."[73] John adds, "But to all who did receive him, who believed in his name, he gave the right to become children of God."[74] From foreigners to fellow citizens! From strangers to adopted children!

At the cross, Jesus secured our adoption into God's family. Those who receive Christ have an eternal inheritance as a child of God. They have a whole new family, with new brothers and sisters. We may not see the richness of this at first because in western cultures family is largely devalued. But in ancient cultures, your family, lineage, and heritage define you. While in our culture we can easily escape from under the shadow of our parents and be known apart from them, in Jesus' day, to know a person you needed to know their family. Because of the cross, we have a new family. We are identified with a new household, a new Father. We are defined by a new lineage and have a new future. We used to be family-less strangers, but now are adopted children of God.

JESUS REMOVES THE WRATH OF GOD

Finally we arrive at the crown jewel: Jesus is our *propitiation*, or wrath-removing sacrifice.[75] Sin is not just a mistake or an unfortunate miscalculation. Sin is an offense against God and the way God intended the world to be (*shalom*). We're often tempted to minimize sin as simply an inadequacy instead of an infraction, but sin is a crime against God and humanity, a vandalism against shalom. Sin is not a mistake, it's evil.

In response to this evil, God rightly feels anger towards us as evil-doers.[76] It's true that God is love, but that's not all that God is. God is also holy, just and righteous. If God wasn't angry with sin and seeking justice, he would cease to be holy and would in fact be immoral. Imagine

---

[73] Galatians 4:4-5
[74] John 1:12-13
[75] Romans 3:25; Hebrews 2:17; I John 2:2; 4:10
[76] Psalm 5:5; 11:5

if God didn't care about the evil that fills our world. What could we say of God if he shrugged his shoulders at rape, violence, drug addiction, exploitation and abuse? *We* rightly get angry at these evils. How much more so the God who is himself righteous and created every human in his image? Imagine how he feels as his beloved creatures, his image-bearers vandalize *shalom* and each other. Tim Keller observes, "the more closely and deeply you love people in your life, the angrier you can get.... The more loving you are, the more ferociously angry you will be at whatever harms your beloved."[77] Because God is so loving, he must be angry at evil—so angry that he must act. He must step in.

My friend Matthew recently found out that a long-time friend of his had been sexually abused as a child. The perpetrator was an older man they both knew and actually lived on the same block as Matthew and his family. Turns out that over the years the friend had told a number of other people about his situation and what he had gone through. Everyone responded the same way. Not wanting to wade into that mess, they each just swept it under the carpet and pretended it wasn't there. When Matthew found out about what had been done, he was angry. It made him angry that an adult would violate and hurt others. It made him angry when the perpetrator admitted what he did, but claimed it wasn't a big deal. It made him angry that so-called friends would ignore the situation and pretend nothing was happening. Matthew, rightfully, was angry. Some people want a God that acts like the so-called friends who simply ignore violence and pretend that no one hurts and nothing evil has happened. The God of the Bible loves us too much to ignore evil and sweep it under the rug. He's not a disinterested god of unloving apathy. He gets angry when shalom is violated. At times, his immense love *requires* anger.

---

[77] Keller, *King's Cross*, 177

So, how does God reconcile his righteous anger at our sin and his great love and mercy? How can God be perfect justice *and* mercy? The answer is found at the cross of Christ. At the cross, God the Father punished God the Son for crimes he did not commit and evils he had not done. God poured out his righteous wrath on Jesus in our place. Though Jesus had done no wrong, he suffered hell on the cross, experiencing isolation from the Father, abandonment, and the wrath of God for our sins.

This was the most critical and painful part of Jesus being on the cross. Thousands of people died on roman crosses. They aren't heroes, but villains. It was a common torture and execution instrument. But what was unique about Jesus' death on the cross was that while dying he suffered the wrath of God for the sins of the world.

In pouring out his wrath and punishment on Jesus, God is able to exercise his perfect justice in punishing all sin perfectly and fairly. No one can object and say that justice wasn't served. The penalty was paid. But since God paid the penalty himself through Christ, God is able to exercise his abundant mercy and forgiveness towards sinners. John writes "In this is love, not that we have loved God but that he loved us and sent his Son to be the propitiation for our sins."[78] Perfect love is seen in the wrath of God for us, being absorbed in the death of Christ for our sins.

On the cross Jesus suffered the hell we deserve for our crimes so that we can experience the grace and mercy of God that Jesus deserved. The cross beautifully displays that God is both justice *and* mercy.

THE COST OF FORGIVENESS

Sometimes people wonder why God can't just declare us forgiven and be done with it. Why the sacrifice? The reality is that forgiveness always

---

[78] I John 4:10

costs. When justice is violated, someone always has to pay. If you were to borrow my car and accidentally damage it, I have two options: I can make you pay it back, in which case I am just and require you to cover the cost of what you've done. Or, I can be merciful and show forgiveness and not require you to cover the cost. But in that case I have to absorb the cost to repair the car. Forgiveness doesn't mean that nobody pays. Forgiveness means that I absorb the cost on your behalf. This is why true forgiveness can be so difficult. As Keller says, "sin always entails a penalty. Guilt can't be dealt with unless someone pays."[79] Forgiveness is never free. It always costs.

The surprising grace of the cross of Jesus—what makes the gospel such good news—is that God chose to absorb the cost himself. He chose the way of forgiveness enduring the great pain of covering the debt through his own sacrifice.

So often we try to be the hero. We try and be good enough. We try and prove ourselves and save ourselves from our suffering. We work hard to make ourselves the hero who rises above and conquers. But we can't do it. The cost is too great. The debt is too big. The offense is too serious. The vandalism is beyond our repair. We need someone to step in our place, to set us free, be our example, make us clean, win our victory, bring reconciliation, secure our adoption, pay our penalty and forgive us our sins. This is so far beyond us. We need a Hero.

---

[79] Keller, *King's Cross*, 101.

Chapter 5
the grand finale

"It ain't over 'til it's over" – Yogi Berra

On the evening of June 15, 2011 100,000 hockey fans crowded Georgia Street in downtown Vancouver to watch on massive screens as their beloved Canucks played in game seven of the Stanley Cup finals. After they lost the game and the series, violence and mayhem erupted on Georgia Street. Cars were overthrown and lit on fire. Shop windows were smashed and stores were looted. Fights broke out in the streets. Anarchy ruled the streets of Vancouver for five hours that night. It was a shocking display of how when unchecked and unaccountable humanity has great potential to cause untold evil.

If Jesus has won victory, defeated death and set us free, why is our world still suffering from the effects of sin? Why is it that when 100,000 people gather on the streets, police aren't concerned about the potential for unplanned and uncontrollable acts of kindness, generosity and good will? Why is our world so marred by cancer, war, famine, abuse and corruption? Why do we suffer at the hand of the very things that Jesus set us free from?

BETWEEN THE AGES

In the story of God we live in this awkward time between the ages. Redemption is now and not yet. The kingdom is here and is coming. Jesus has truly forgiven us, cleansed us and set us free and he has truly conquered Satan, sin and death. And yet, while that victory has been won, and God's kingdom has been inaugurated, it has not yet come to fullness. We still long for and await the full consummation of the victory of God in Jesus.

On the cross, Jesus defeated death forever. Death is dead. For those who are in Christ, death has lost its sting forever.[80] Death is now powerless. When Jesus paid the penalty for our sin, death lost its teeth. Instead of a 600 lb Siberian tiger, death has been made into a domesticated and declawed house cat. It can no longer harm. And so, death is no longer something to be feared. And yet, we all still die. Death is defeated, but it is still our reality. Why is that?

Jesus' victory over death was won at the cross, and yet we still await its full consummation. Death is dead now, but we look forward to the complete fulfillment in the new heavens and new earth when God "will wipe away every tear from their eyes, and death shall be no more, neither shall there be mourning nor crying nor pain anymore, for the former things have passed away."[81] Death and sadness pass away. Now that's a funeral I'd like to attend. Forget the tuna sandwiches, let's throw a feast! Death is dead!

---

[80] I Corinthians 15:55-57
[81] Revelation 21:4

The same could be said about our sin. Because of the cross of Jesus Christ, the sin of everyone who is in Christ has been completely atoned for. The penalty is paid. The debt is forgiven. The stains are made clean.

And yet, we still sin, don't we? We may be forgiven, but we aren't free from sin. We still fail. We still rebel. We still sin. We are positionally holy, but in our experience we are still a work in progress. We are forgiven now, but we long for the day when sin will be eradicated forever, and our hearts will be so fully changed that our desire will always and only be for God. In the new heavens and new earth "nothing unclean will ever enter it" and "no longer will there be anything accursed, but the throne of God and of the Lamb will be in it, and his servants will worship him."[82] We are positionally holy right now, but on that day we will be experientially holy as well. We will become what we are.

And though Jesus disarmed and defeated evil on the cross, there continues to be evil, suffering and injustice in our world. Why is it that so often in our world the words of Green Day ring true, "nice guys finish last"? Cheaters often prosper. Liars get ahead in life.

But while it seems that injustice reigns, because of the victory of Jesus we know that there will be perfect justice in the end. God wins. Evil loses.

In one of Jesus' parables, he explains how the world is like a field that has both wheat and weeds growing up together. Knowing that removing the weeds while the wheat is still growing could cause harm to the wheat, the farmer allows both the wheat and weeds to continue together until harvest time when the reapers will then gather the weeds and burn them, and *then* harvest the wheat. Jesus explains that the defeated kingdom of evil will continue alongside the kingdom of God until the time of judgment when evil will be defeated forever.[83] While often life seem

---

[82] Revelation 21:27; 22:3
[83] Matthew 13:24-30, 36-43

unjust now, there will be a day of perfect justice when evil will be punished and righteousness will reign forever.

THE RESTORATION OF *SHALOM*

When Adam and Eve rebelled and trusted the lies of the serpent rather
than the truth of God, they were expelled out of their garden paradise
and *shalom* was lost. But by God's grace, his story is a u-shaped story. It
starts and ends with *shalom*. In the very good beginning, the first man
and the first woman enjoy God's good creation in paradise, free from
sin, shame and death. The story of the Bible is the long and painful
journey of a gracious and sovereign God bringing his people back to
the garden via the cross.

At the end of the story, humanity returns to the garden, but this
time, the garden is a beautiful garden *city*.[84] Heaven has come down to
earth. Everything is made new and the curse of sin is gone forever. This
is not some nebulous, disembodied existence in a cloudy place like a
commercial for Philly cream cheese. When you think of heaven, don't
picture harps, wings and clouds. God will renew the *earth* and restore
shalom. We'll experience life on earth without sin, shame or death. We'll
experience life as it was meant to be with "universal flourishing, wholeness and delight."[85]

This new age will be ushered in with a huge wedding feast, complete
with rich food and good wine to celebrate the union of Jesus with his
bride, the church.[86] We're told that in that day lambs will be able to lie
down with wolves, knowing they won't be torn to shreds. Just to belabor
the point to death we're told the same thing about goats with leopards,

---

[84] Revelation 21:1-22:5
[85] Plantinga Jr., *Not the Way It's Supposed to Be*, 10.
[86] Isaiah 25:6-9; Matthew 26:29; Revelation 19:6-9

calves with lions, cows with bears, and children with snakes.[87] With no need for war anymore, people will convert their weapons into farming equipment. Isaiah pictures how everyone will "beat their swords into plowshares, and their spears into pruning hooks."[88] In that line of thinking, Richard Mouw pictures intercontinental ballistic missile silos being converted into training tanks for scuba divers.[89] There will still be work, as there was before sin, but it will be free of the frustration and futility that was introduced with the curse. Likewise, we'll still rest, but it will be the deeply satisfying and invigorating rest that escapes us so often in our high-octane overly-caffeinated culture. It will be life as it was meant to be: free from sin, suffering and death. Life lived for God's glory, enjoying him all of our days.

After the climax in J.R.R. Tolkein's *The Lord of the Rings*, Samwise Gamgee awakens and is shocked to see Gandalf, realizing that his friend wasn't dead as he believed. With open mouth, filled with both bewilderment and great joy, Sam finally gasps, "Gandalf! I thought you were dead! But then I thought I was dead myself. Is everything sad going to come untrue?" Tim Keller adds, "The answer of Christianity to that question is – yes. Everything sad is going to come untrue and it will somehow be *greater* for having once been broken and lost."[90] The hope of the gospel is that all that has been broken, lost and corrupted because of sin will become untrue.

---

[87] Isaiah 11:6-7
[88] Isaiah 2:4
[89] Richard J. Mouw, *When the Kings Come Marching In: Isaiah and the New Jerusalem* (Grand Rapids, MI: William B. Eerdmans, 1983), 19-20. As quoted in Plantinga Jr., *Not the Way Its Supposed to Be,* 11.
[90] Timothy Keller, *The Reason for God: Belief in an Age of Skepticism* (New York: Dutton, 2008), 33.

KINGDOM COME

In this awkward, between-the-ages time that we find ourselves in, we need to remember the victory that Jesus has already won and look forward to the full consummation of that victory in the coming age. This is perhaps best exemplified in the way Jesus taught us to pray: "Your kingdom come, your will be done, on earth as it is in heaven."[91] God already reigns in perfect justice and righteousness in heaven. His will is always done in heaven. Our hope and prayer now, is for the day when God's reign will come and fill the whole earth as well. We pray for the day when heaven comes to earth, justice is exacted, righteousness fills the earth, and God's glory shines forth in perfection. We long for and pray for life as God intended it to be. Come Lord Jesus.

---

[91] Matthew 6:10

PART TWO
living in God's story

entering the story

"Christ Jesus has made me his own" - Apostle Paul

What's the story that defines your life? Who's the hero of your story? Everyone understands their existence within some kind of meta-narrative, a grand story of the world you find yourself in. In part one, we saw that the story of God is told in four parts: creation, fall, redemption and restoration. Jesus is the ultimate Hero of God's story. This story is not simply facts for us to give assent to, it is the story that must define our life. We need to understand our existence and live our lives in response to the truth of the story of God.

While part one reviewed the story of God, in part two we unpack how we are to live in response to God' story. The gospel is a not a "ticket to heaven", but is life-altering news. The gospel changes everything.

Chapter 6

the gospel opposes religion

"Grace. It's a name for a girl.
It's also a thought that changed the world" – Grace by U2

One of my favorite stories of all time is *Les Misérables* by Victor Hugo. In the very first few chapters, the notorious Jean Valjean is released from prison and on his journey he happens upon a town where he is refused lodging at every turn. Having to declare that he is a convict, none will have him. He's even refused in the town prison. Eventually he happens upon the bishop's house and to Valjean's great surprise, he is not turned away but is taken in, served dinner on the bishop's finest china, and given a warm bed for the night. What generosity and grace!

With a full stomach and warm bed, Jean Valjean awakens in the middle of the night, capable only of thinking about the value of the silver that was used for dinner. Hugo writes, "those six silver plates took possession of him."[92] Unable to sleep or rest his thoughts elsewhere, he quietly gets up, locates the silver, stuffs it in his sack, jumps out the

---

[92] Victor Hugo, *Les Misérables* (New York: Simon & Schuster, 1964), 24.

window and leaves.

The next morning, after eating his breakfast off wooden dishes, the good bishop notices four men approaching his home. The local police have captured Jean Valjean in his escape! The reader naturally anticipates a scene where the bishop scolds Valjean for trampling upon his generosity and stealing the silver. Is this how he repays their grace and good favor? The old bishop rushes up to Valjean and says "But I gave you the candlesticks also, which are silver like the rest and would bring two hundred francs. Why did you not take them along with your plates?"[93] The guards, at this point, are thoroughly confused having assumed that Valjean stole the silver—as, indeed, he did. But the bishop *insists* that Valjean has stolen nothing, and he sends him on his way with the silver candlesticks as well.

Jean Valjean, an undeserving recipient of generosity, should have been arrested for stealing silver from the bishop. But, instead, his wicked acts were repaid with more generosity and mercy. As the story progresses, that experience of grace, was so radical and transformational that over the course of the story Jean Valjean, reflecting on that grace, is changed from a hardened, wicked criminal with no respect for life, to a soft, gentle, loving person who will sacrifice his own life for others.

ALL THE NEWS THAT'S FIT TO PRINT

The word gospel means "good news". When Christians talk about the gospel, they mean the good news about the death and resurrection of Jesus Christ and its implications for us. A gospel is a proclamation of an event that has happened in history that changes our status now. Keller writes, "Right there you can see the difference between Christianity and

---

[93] Ibid., 29.

all other religions, including no religion. The essence of other religions is advice; Christianity is essentially news."[94] While other religions teach you a list of things to do to earn you God's favour, Christianity is an announcement that the work is done. The gospel is the joyful news that the life, death and resurrection of Jesus has earned God's favour for us. There's nothing left to do, it's already been done.

This was the life-altering message of the early church. As the Apostles proclaimed the gospel they were proclaiming the good news about what Jesus had already accomplished. They weren't giving advice but proclaiming news. The preaching of the early church was a continual re-telling of the amazing story of what God had done through Jesus Christ.

"Let all... know for certain that God has made him both Lord and Christ, this Jesus whom you crucified."[95]

"The God of our fathers, glorified his servant Jesus, whom you delivered over and denied in the presence of Pilate."[96]

"There is salvation in no one else, for there is no other name under heaven given among men by which we must be saved."[97]

"The God of our fathers raised Jesus, whom you killed by hanging him on a tree. God exalted him at his right hand as Leader and Savior, to give repentance to Israel and forgiveness of sins."[98]

Over and over again, the church proclaimed the news of what was accomplished by God through Jesus Christ. At its very core, Christian faith is not about what you do, but about what Jesus has done. It's not advice to live a better life, but news about the perfect life that was already lived.

---

[94] Keller, *King's Cross*, 15.
[95] Acts 2:36
[96] Acts 3:13
[97] Acts 4:12
[98] Acts 5:30-31

The apostle Paul summarizes this good news as he writes to the church in Corinth, "I would remind you, brothers, of the gospel... that Christ died for our sins in accordance with the Scriptures, that he was buried, that he was raised on the third day in accordance with the Scriptures, and that he appeared to Cephas, then to the twelve."[99] The good news is that Jesus lived a perfectly righteous life, died as a substitute for our sins, rose to new life defeating sin and death, and lives today as King forever. The good news is that because of the cross, God gives us grace instead of judgment, life instead of death, hope instead of despair, wholeness instead of shame, and freedom instead of bondage. Like Jean Valjean, our evil deeds and our selfish hearts are repaid with generosity, forgiveness and new life.

THE DANGER OF RELIGION

It's of absolute importance that we distinguish the gospel from both religion and irreligion. Frequently the mistake is made to identify the message of the gospel as another religion, but Jesus simply won't allow us to confuse the two. Religion is about obeying certain rules, believing certain truths and doing certain things in order to gain favour with God. Like the scholar who came to test Jesus, religion asks "what shall I *do* to inherit eternal life?"[100] The emphasis is all on performance. Religion is about working hard enough, earning enough that God will *have to* reward you. Religion is the pursuit of putting God in your debt. Freedom is sought through doing so much good that God owes you.

But in the end, religion will always lead to either pride or despair. If you manage to trick yourself into believing you truly are good enough for God's favour, you won't be able to help feeling superior to others.

---

[99] I Corinthians 15:1, 3-5
[100] Luke 10:25

Pride will overtake you. Since you keep all the rules better than other people, how can you not look down on those who don't keep the same rules as you? Arrogance is inevitable.

Or if you are given the rare gift of self-awareness and recognize that you will never be truly good, you will never keep all the rules, you will never earn righteousness, you will inevitably be overcome with despair, being without hope on your own. Once you realize that you will never achieve the moral standards expected of you, how can you not feel overwhelmed by your plight and fall into despair and hopelessness? Religion doesn't bring life, it kills life and leads to either pride or despair.

Irreligion on the other hand, is about disregarding all rules and living for self. Irreligion embraces sin and emphasizes self-indulgence. Freedom is sought through selfishness and disregard for all authority. Irreligion is all about trampling on God's grace and rewarding yourself now. In the end, irreligion will always lead to emptiness and dissatisfaction. When the gods we pursue prove themselves to be liars and their promises to be empty, we are left joyless, purposeless and discontented.

Jesus repeatedly shows his followers that both ways lead to slavery and death. As Keller puts it Jesus says that "both the irreligious and the religious are spiritually lost, both life-paths are dead ends, and that every thought the human race has had about how to connect to God has been wrong."[101] Jesus has not come to teach religion. Religion is the problem, not the solution.

The gospel is the answer to both religion and irreligion. The gospel is "the power of God for salvation to everyone who believes"[102] for both the religious and irreligious. While religion and irreligion focus on the things you *do*, the gospel cuts straight to the heart. Both religion

---

[101] Timothy Keller, *The Prodigal God: Recovering the Heart of the Christian Faith* (New York: Dutton, 2008), 10-11.
[102] Romans 1:16

and irreligion are obsessed with behavior—moral and immoral, respectively—the gospel is concerned with heart motivation and affections. As we identify with Jesus and find our hope in his substitutionary death for us, we are given new hearts with new affections and desires. Our values and passions change. Paul writes, "If anyone is in Christ, he is a new creation. The old has passed away; behold the new has come."[103] Though we were born spiritually dead, we have been made alive in Christ.[104] **Paul** emphasizes "this is not your own doing; it is the gift of God."[105] By God's grace, he changes our hearts and makes us into new creatures—born again, as Jesus put it—with new motives, new affections and new desires. Religion can never change hearts, it can only modify outward behavior. Even the most vile person can act nicely with selfish motives. Religion is behavior modification through hard work, but the gospel is a heart transplant by God's grace.

One of my favorite theologians, Bono, puts it this way, "I really believe we've moved out of the realm of Karma into one of Grace." He explains, "at the center of all religions is the idea of Karma. You know, what you put out comes back to you: an eye for an eye, a tooth for a tooth, or in physics every action is met by an equal or an opposite one. It's clear to me that Karma is at the very heart of the Universe."

Then he says, "yet, along comes this idea called Grace to upend all that 'as you reap, so will you sow' stuff. Grace defies reason and logic. Love interrupts, if you like, the consequences of your actions, which in my case is very good news indeed, because I've done a lot of stupid stuff."

He then concludes, "I'd be in big trouble if Karma was going to finally be my judge... It doesn't excuse my mistakes, but I'm holding

---

[103] 2 Corinthians 5:17
[104] Ephesians 2:1, 4–6
[105] Ephesians 2:8

out for Grace. I'm holding out that Jesus took my sins onto the Cross, because I know who I am, and I hope I don't have to depend on my own religiosity."[106]

Bono recognizes that religion offers no hope. Religion is built on the premise of karma, where everyone gets what they deserve. This may sound attractive at first, but it's the furthest thing from good news! Karma is very bad news. The last thing we want is karma, what we need is grace, grace given to us because of the cross.

TRUE REPENTANCE

The salvation of the gospel cannot be earned or deserved. It is not a religion. Salvation is not something to be accomplished. It is purely a gift of grace from God. The gospel, in essence, is news reporting what has already happened, how recent events have changed life forever. The gospel is never earned, but we do need to respond to it. We need to receive the gift. The only way to do that is through *repentance* and *faith*. These aren't acts that we do to earn salvation by any means. Rather, they are means of receiving what is already earned.

I think of repentance in three parts. First is the feeling of godly sorrow for our sin. We say *godly* sorrow, because there are two kinds of sorrow. Paul explains, "Godly sorrow brings repentance that leads to salvation and leaves no regret, but worldly sorrow brings death."[107] Godly sorrow is an abhorring of our sin, a deep regret at our wrong. Worldly sorrow is a sorrow at getting caught.

Worldly sorrow is the sorrow we see expressed when a famous athlete or politician gets caught in a sex scandal. After full and adamant

---

[106] Michka Assayas, *Bono: In Conversation with Michka Assayas* (New York: Riverhead Books, 2005), 203-204.
[107] 2 Corinthians 7:10, NIV

denial of any wrongdoing until the weight of the evidence won't allow for that gambit any longer, they finally come out—at the urging of their public relations team—looking their best, tears and all, for a carefully worded public apology. With admitting wrong, they apologize for causing hurt and letting down their supporters. They usually blame some kind of lapse in judgment that was completely out of character. They're a good person, who by some weird succession of events accidentally did something that may have hurt someone, allegedly.[108] This is not repentance. This is not true sorrow. This is what Paul calls "worldly sorrow", a sorrow for consequences, but not for actions. We, on the other hand, are called to godly sorrow, a true feeling of remorse, not that we have to suffer through consequences, but a remorse for the wrong that we have done. We have sinned and we abhor it.

The second part of repentance is confession. After feeling that godly sorrow, we need to admit our guilt. We need to name our sin. We do this with our kids, don't we? It's not enough if my son mutters an apology, I want him to confess that what he did was wrong. So I ask, what are you sorry for? I'm drawing out a confession. He needs to identify his behaviour as wrong and to admit guilt. A general apology that is sorry for nothing in particular is not being sorry at all. Our default response in life is to claim innocence and declare ourselves not guilty. Confession is to enter a guilty plea before God.

Cease the counter-arguments. Fire the defence lawyers. Quit the negotiations. Admit guilt. No more spin. No more blame-shifting. No more games. Own your sin. Admit your guilt. This is godly confession.

Finally, repentance is also an act of turning. It's a change of stance, a u-turn, a reversal of direction. It's both a turning *away* from sin and

---

[108] For an excellent analysis of self-justification see Carol Tavris and Elliot Aronson, *Mistakes Were Made (But Not By Me): Why We Justify Foolish Behaviours, Bad Decisions, and Hurtful Acts* (Orlando, FL: Harcourt, 2007).

a turning *towards* Jesus Christ. It's not true repentance to feel sorrow, name your sin, and then cling to it as tight as ever. Repentance forsakes our own behaviour and turns to Christ instead. Earlier we said that sin was the exchange of the truth about God for a lie and the worship of created things (idolatry) rather than the Creator.[109] Repentance is reversing that exchange. It's a rejection of the lie and returning to the truth. It's the act of letting go our death grip on our idols and turning to worship God instead. Repentance feels godly sorrow, confesses wrong, and turns away from sin and toward Jesus Christ. J.I. Packer writes, "Repentance is more than just sorrow for the past; repentance is a change of mind and heart, a new life of denying self and serving the Savior as king in self's place."[110]

Ultimately, repentance is only possible through the grace of God. When the apostles saw that many gentiles had responded to the gospel, they said "then to the Gentiles also God has granted repentance that leads to life."[111] God grants repentance. We experience godly sorrow only as the Holy Spirit convicts us of our sin, which otherwise we would be ignorant of. God grants us by his grace the ability to confess our sin and to turn away from it towards Christ. Repentance is a gift of God.

TRUE FAITH

Faith is trust that Jesus and Jesus alone can save us. We stop trusting in our own righteousness and moral performance and place our trust that Jesus' death and resurrection paid the full penalty for our sin and credited us with his righteousness. In faith, I stop building a case for my own righteousness. I give up that futile pursuit and place my trust in Christ's

---

[109] Romans 1:25
[110] J.I. Packer, *Evangelism and the Sovereignty of God* (Downers Grove, IL: Intervarsity Press, 1991), 71.
[111] Acts 11:18

substitutionary death and his perfect righteousness. In faith, we rest in the gospel story and live with Jesus as the Hero of our story, finding our identity in who we are in Christ.

Faith is believing that Jesus was who he said he was and that he did what he said he did. Faith believes that Jesus is the way, the truth and the life, the only way to the Father, that he truly did die as a substitute for our sins, that he truly did rise from death, conquering Satan, sin and death forever. Faith believes that Jesus reigns as king forever and will return to consummate the kingdom of God and bring justice and righteousness to the earth.

It's important to clarify that it is not the *act* of faith that saves, but the *object* of faith. It's not the intensity, purity or boldness of faith that achieves salvation, but it is the achievements of the one in whom you place your faith. A.W. Tozer said,

> Faith is not in itself a meritorious act; the merit is in the One toward Whom it is directed. Faith is a redirecting of our sight, a getting out of the focus of our own vision and getting God into focus.... Faith looks out instead of in and the whole life falls into line.[112]

Salvation is not for those who have a strong faith, but for those who have faith in a strong saviour.

THE STORY OF GOD CALLS US TO RESPOND

God has created you in his own image, designed with purpose and dignity. And though you have rebelled against God and made him your enemy, he has loved you and pursued you. He made a way for salvation, absorbing the cost of forgiveness himself, making a way for

---

[112] A.W. Tozer, *The Pursuit of God: Finding the Divine in the Everyday* (Radford, VA: Wilder Publications, 2008), 60.

reconciliation. And now he is calling you to trade in your story for his. He's calling you to abandon your childish attempts at being the hero and writing your own story for your own glory. Repent of your religion and irreligion. Place your faith in the True Hero, a real Saviour. Come and live in the story of God.

chapter 7

the gospel remakes our identity

"The way to be truly happy is to be truly human, and the way to be truly human is to be truly godly." – J.I. Packer

Very few of us work for money. Most work for value, identity and significance. We work in order to gain influence, success and power. We work to accomplish something and gain recognition for our abilities. We work to earn security, build an empire, or fulfill our desires. We work to carve out a better identity for ourselves. If we only worked for money, we wouldn't have invented the smartphone. There's nothing inherently wrong about getting email 24/7, but for many of us it may be a strong indicator that we define ourselves by what we do.

This is evident in how we introduce ourselves. You can learn a lot about a stranger by the words that immediately follow their name. When introducing themselves, what are the important need-to-know facts? What's the one thing that this stranger feels we should know about them? For most people that all-important fact is the nature of their oc- cupation. Our careers have come to define us.

The call of the gospel is not to give assent to a few theological facts, but to radically re-centre our lives around Jesus. Our story becomes re-written around the story of God.

IT'S GOSPEL ALL THE WAY

Often Christians think of the gospel as the entry point into Christian life. The gospel is how you "get in." But then we quickly move past the gospel to moral living and obedience. But as common as this thought is, it simply isn't accurate. As Tim Keller has frequently said, the gospel is not the ABCs of Christianity, it's the A-Z. We *never* outgrow the gospel. We never grow past it or graduate beyond it. We never stop needing the gospel.

The gospel is not only our entry point into Christian faith, it's also the way we grow in Christ and persevere until the end. Paul tells the Colossian church "therefore, as you received Christ Jesus the Lord, so walk in him."[113] They are to walk or live or continue in Christ, just as they received Him. The Christian life is one of walking in the gospel. To move beyond the gospel is not maturity, but immaturity. The mature and healthy are those who still cling tightly to the simple but profound truths of the gospel and place their whole identity in the gospel story.

Martin Luther launched the protestant reformation when he nailed his *95 Theses* to the door of Castle Church in Wittenburg. He began that important work by saying "When our Lord and Master, Jesus Christ, said 'Repent', He called for the entire life of believers to be one of repentance." Our entire life? This sounds bleak, as if we will never make progress and will continually be stuck at stage one. But as Tim Keller explains, "[Luther] was saying that repentance is the way we make

---

[113] Colossians 2:6

progress in the Christian life. Indeed, pervasive, all-of-life repentance is the best sign that we are growing deeply and rapidly into the character of Jesus."[114] Repentance is not the enemy of growth, but the agent for it. We grow in maturity through a daily rhythm of gospel-grounded re-pentance, re-finding our identity in the gospel story and re-establishing our trust in Christ alone.

IDENTITY

The gospel story is not just about avoiding hell. It's not as much about a change in destination as it is about a change in identity. The apostle Paul puts it like this, "I have been crucified with Christ. It is no longer I who live, but Christ who lives in me. And the life I now live in the flesh I live by faith in the Son of God, who loved me and gave himself for me."[115] He's saying, I'm not the same person. The old me, the one wracked with sin, is dead and gone. He went to the cross with Jesus Christ. The new me isn't so much me, but Christ within me. I've undergone a whole change in identity, an identity now radically re-shaped around the gospel.

Elsewhere, while talking about attaining the future resurrection, Paul writes, "Not that I have already obtained this or am already perfect, but I press on to make it my own, because Christ Jesus has made me his own."[116] Christ Jesus has made me his own. Upon their meeting, Jesus has completely taken over Paul. Paul was writing his life story, but as Jared Wilson puts it, Jesus stole his pen. He was hijacked by the gospel. Apprehended by Jesus. Paul didn't receive Jesus *into* his life. Jesus isn't that passive, and he's not into sharing. Instead, Jesus made Paul his own.

---

[114] Timothy Keller, "All of Life is Repentance", 2000 [online], available from http://download. redeemer.com/pdf/learn/resources/All_of_Life_Is_Repentance-Keller.pdf
[115] Galatians 2:20; See also Romans 6:6 and Galatians 6:14
[116] Philippians 3:12

"You're mine now. You belonged to death, but now you belong to me."

This new identity becomes the basis for any moral exhortation. Paul writes, "Do not lie to one another, seeing that you have put off the old self with its practices and have put on the new self, which is being renewed in knowledge after the image of its creator."[117] Christians shouldn't lie because lying is an attribute of the old identity and is contrary to our new gospel-shaped identity. Lying isn't who we are anymore. It used to be, but now we have a new identity which is being shaped to image (or mirror) our Creator. We're not commanded to stop lying *so that* we earn God's approval. Rather, we stop lying because it's incompatible with our new gospel-shaped identity in the image of God. It's not who we are anymore as a new creation.

We need to derive our worth and value, not from our performance, role or relationships, but from our position in Christ as reconciled sinners. Our core identity is with Jesus Christ. The gospel defines us. Instead of telling our own story, our lives tell the gospel story. But this new gospel identity is unnatural for us. We find it much easier to build our identity on what we do, who we know or what we have than to build it on our position in Christ. We like telling our own story very much, thank you. Sin works in humans to distort our identity and to find our value in places other than Christ. Here are some common ways we exchange the truth for a lie and distort our identity:[118]

PERFORMANCE

In the distortion of performance we wrongly build our identity on what we do—our accomplishments, morality, success or abilities—rather

---

[117] Colossians 3:9-10
[118] For these ideas on identity distortions I'm indebted to Pastor Bill Clem's Re:Train class on discipleship.

than on who we are in Christ. We believe the lie that I am what I do. We define ourselves by our works. This performance distortion can play out in some very different ways. The distortion of performance is seen in the workaholic businessman who sacrifices 60, 70 or 80 hours a week at the feet of his work/god, or in the hard-working athlete that does anything and everything to win, believing it will vindicate his existence. When Rocky's girlfriend asks him why it's so important that he go the distance in the fight, he responds, "then I'll know I'm not a bum." Tim Keller surmises that Rocky "looked to athletic achievement as the defining force that gave meaning to [his life]."[119] But this performance-based identity is also evident in the pious Christian who serves others, gives generously, attends church, and does a thousand other good things all motivated by *self-righteousness*. This was the toxic behavior of the Pharisees who Jesus so often exposed and criticized. They emphasized appearances, performance and track record over heart motivations and repentance. An identity built on performance—even moral performance—is a distortion of our true identity and is toxic.

But performance-based identity distortions are not reserved for workaholic businessmen and star athletes. The stay-at-home mom can distort her identity by finding her worth in the quantity and quality of the children she is raising. A sort of justification by childbearing. Meanwhile, those who are unable to have children somehow feel less than human, as if made less in the image of God. The homeschooling mother of five may derive her worth from the superior performance of her children—whether academic or athletic—in the same way that the wealthy investor builds his personal value on the performance of his stocks. We are all tempted to build our identity on what we do.

---

[119] Keller, *Reason for God*, 162.

Instead of finding our worth in our own performance, we need to build our identity on what *Christ* has accomplished for us. We need to trade in the deceptive lie of "I am what I do" for the glorious truth of "I am what Christ has done". The truth is that all my efforts add up to nothing before God. My moral performance doesn't impress God. Even on my best days, I am still a rebellious sinner entirely dependent on the mercy of God for life. My justification comes not from my achievements but from the cross. Jesus lived the perfectly righteous life that I was required to live, but could not live. He died the death that I deserve as justice for my sinful life. My standing before God is based on Christ's sacrifice and perfect performance, not mine. Paul says, "For by grace you have been saved through faith. And this is not your own doing; it is the gift of God, not a result of works, so that no one may boast."[120] Salvation is a gift received, not an accomplishment earned. Why? To eliminate boasting. When we understand our identity rightly, we can only boast about Jesus and never ourselves. The cross eliminates all performance-driven identity distortions.

As a hard-working pastor I am continually tempted by this distortion. I'm tempted to find my worth in the success of my sermons, the effectiveness of my writing or the growth in my church. I feel vindicated when a controversial decision I make proves to have been the right one. Likewise, when a sermon fails or a meeting goes bad, I come home sulking. What is that? When my outlook is affected by my performance I'm believing the lie that I am what I do. When I perform well, I feel vindicated, alive and significant. When I perform poorly, I feel worthless, depressed and am tempted to quit. When my attitude fluctuates with my performance I am disbelieving the truth that my justification is based on Christ's perfect righteousness and not my own. My failure to believe that

---

[120] Ephesians 2:8-9

truth distorts my view. I need to repent of my desire to perform and instead daily rebuild my identity on the gospel story.

FAILURE

The distortion of failure is the similar, but opposite error. Here, a person defines themselves by their sin and wrongdoing: I am what I've done wrong. This distortion is also based on *doing* instead of *being*, but now builds an identity on the wrongdoing of the present or past. We can allow our sins to define our entire existence so that outside of our sin we have no identity. While there is much to be commended about Alcoholics Anonymous and other twelve step recovery programs, I wonder if, out of a desire to fight denial and encourage confession, participants fall into the distortion of failure. "My name is Steve and I'm an alcoholic." I am what I've done.

I met with a Christian woman who confessed that about fifteen years earlier she had had an abortion. We could get into the circumstances around it and who all shared blame, but the important piece is that even though she had repented of this wrong act and had sought God's forgiveness, all these years later she still defined herself by her wrongdoing. I'm not for a second vindicating her behavior or suggesting abortion is anything less than sinful. But for this woman, she had shaped her identity around her sin instead of around Jesus. In so doing, she failed to (truly) believe the gospel in some important ways. She rightly believed herself to be a sinner, but she failed to define herself by the forgiveness of God and the cleansing of her sins by the cross of Jesus Christ.

The lie is that I am what I've done wrong. My failure defines me. The truth is that I am a forgiven sinner. We need to remember and believe the gospel and build our identity on the truth of the gospel story. I am created in God's image and therefore have worth, dignity and value as an image-bearer of God, period. Though I am a broken and sinful person, who has done and is capable of doing incredible evil, I am now redeemed, forgiven, clean, whole and new because of Jesus Christ. We need to remember the truth that "as far as the east is from the west, so far does [God] remove our transgressions from us."[121] We don't deny the existence of our sin, but its location. My sin is great, but it has been removed from me and laid on Christ. I no longer wear my sin, but I now wear the perfect righteousness of Christ.

SUFFERING

Sometimes we are affected more by the sins committed against us than by those we commit ourselves. The distortion of suffering is the temptation to build our identity on the evil that has been done against me. I define myself by how I have been abused, victimized and the sinful things done to me. For instance, victims of sexual abuse may view themselves as dirty and unworthy of love, even disgusted at themselves.[122] Victims of abuse often feel worthless and deserving of such treatment. They accept their abuse as normal and will pass on their hurt and destruction to others, entering a cycle of pain and abuse. Sin makes us filthy. It defiles us and brings us shame. Those who have been sinned against will naturally feel dirty and unlovable. This feeling betrays their true identity in Christ.

The truth is that if you in are in Christ, you are clean and whole and pure. God says to you: "though your sins are like scarlet, they shall be as white as snow; though they are red like crimson, they shall become like wool."[123] Jesus has removed the filth, shame and uncleanness that we

---

[121] Psalm 103:12
[122] Holcomb and Holcomb, *Rid of My Disgrace*, 72.
[123] Isaiah 1:18

experience from both the sins we commit and the sins committed against us. You are no longer defined by your suffering, but by the tender mercy of God for you. His gentle cleansing grace is what defines you. You are pure and new in Christ.

ROLES AND RELATIONSHIPS

For many people, their worth and significance are derived from their place in society or the influence they have. They are defined by who they know and who knows them. It's their importance in the community or the importance of their role or responsibilities that give them value as a person. We see this distortion amongst name-dropping politicians and civic leaders. But we also can see it amongst stay at home moms who find their worth in being needed by everyone and being the reliable one that holds it all together. This distortion is evidenced in a proud church ministry leader or a socialite who is rich in image only, both of whom see themselves as someone who really matters (I mean really, *really* matters).

So everyone knows your name, does God? You know a lot of people, are you known by God?

The truth is that for those who are in Christ the greatest relationship they have is with God himself. Being known by God the Father makes the masses seem dull and inconsequential. We need to recognize that we have value as image-bearers of God and find our identity in being adopted into God's family. We don't need to win friends and gain popularity. We don't need to spin our image and create influence. We have worth and value in our relationship with God. We don't need a powerful job with an impressive title to be a person of consequence. Because of the gospel, you have a God-ordained position to work in the kingdom of God as a humble servant of the King. The person who's life is shaped by the gospel story is free from the slavery of people-pleasing and is able to joyfully work for King Jesus.

DISTORTIONS DISTORTIONS EVERYWHERE

Countless young men refuse to grow up and take responsibility, but would rather pursue one thrilling experience after another, having built an identity on what they've experienced rather than on what God has called them to do.

I have a friend who won't let his kids play on the hardwood floor. They got a new couch, but the kids can't sit on it. Everything has to look perfect. Always. His identity is resting on it. Buddy, put the idol down and play with your kids.

In the TV show *The Mentalist*, the lead character Patrick Jane obsessively pursues Red John, the man who murdered his wife and daughter. His anger and hatred consumes him. Without his need for vengeance, he is nothing.

If the gospel doesn't shape our identity, we can fall into any number of other distortions as well, quickly forgetting that no matter who we are, what we've done or what's been done to us, we are valuable as image-bearers of God, redeemed sinners, cleansed by his grace and adopted into his family. This is the root of much of our sin and struggle, a failure to truly believe the gospel story and build our identity on it.

The story of God calls us not just to a new future, but a new present. You are a new creation, a new person with a new identity, new meaning. Don't continue to rebuild your identity on those same tired distortions. Trade in the lie for the truth and find your meaning in God's story. The story of God is inviting you in.

chapter 8

the gospel shapes us into community

"By this all people will know that you are my disciples, if you have love for one another." – Jesus

I recently received an out of the blue phone call from a woman named Elizabeth. She was an older woman who lived on her own and was looking for help with cooking and cleaning as she was unable to do this for herself anymore. What she needed was to move into a care home or assisted living facility, and I was able to connect her with a place in our area. But what shocked me through our conversation was how alone she was. She was married for over 30 years, but is now alone (not sure if it was through death or divorce). Elizabeth and her husband chose to not have any kids. She only had one sister and they haven't been on speaking terms in years. No husband. No kids. No grandkids. No brothers or sisters (that will speak to her). No nephews or nieces. No friends. No one. Sure, there are community nurses and social workers that help her out, but she has no community.

This is not the way it's supposed to be! In Genesis 2:18, after God had created the first man, but before sin entered the world, God observed Adam—his good creation, in his good world—and concluded, "It is *not good* that the man should be alone; I will make him a helper fit for him."[124] We have a built-in need for community, for belonging and relationship. This is not part of the brokenness of the world, but part of our creation. Being human means being made for community. This is one of the ways we image God. God is a Trinity—Father, Son and Holy Spirit—a perfect three-in-one community. As God is a community, he made us for community as well.

I think that this is one of the reasons why around the globe, we love professional sports so much. Why do we get so crazy about sports? It seems it's always been this way, whether it was Roman chariot racing in the Circus Maximus, which could seat up to 250,000 people, to thousands of vuvuzela-blowing fans during World Cup frenzy in South Africa, to the record 111 million people who watched the Packers beat the Steelers in Super Bowl XLV in 2011. As people created for community, we love to be part of something bigger than ourselves, to be part of a crowd of thousands united in a common mission and vision for our team. My own beloved Vancouver Canucks recently ran with this theme by using the slogan "we are all Canucks." They sought to create a sense of belonging and community for the entire city. The Canucks aren't a team of 23 players but a community of 2 million fans. We were created with a longing for community and connectedness, to be part of a movement much bigger than our individual selves.

SHOPPING WITH JESUS

Sadly, Christianity in North America has been significantly influenced by

---

[124] Genesis 2:18, emphasis mine.

western individualistic consumerism.[125] Most think of their Christianity as a personal thing between "me and Jesus." We talk of Jesus being your *personal* Lord and Saviour, and ask people if they know God *personally*. Many Christians possess an overly-individualized faith. They like Jesus, but aren't so sure about Jesus' people.

Church members complain that the music was too loud, too quiet, too old-fashioned, too new, and not *exactly* the way they wanted it. We complain about the teaching being too long and boring, as well as too short, trite and unbiblical. If the passage confronts our most cherished sins, we accuse the preacher of being a bully. If the passage confronts other people's sins, we applaud the preacher for "telling it like it is." We complain about the seats, that the (free) coffee is bad and the cups are too small. It may be with uplifted fist and bulging veins, or simply in the quiet of our bitter hearts, but we so often complain whenever we don't get our way. It wouldn't be Sunday lunch without roast beef and gossip.

Often this overly-individualistic Christianity produces a religious consumerism. Churches function as purveyors of spiritual goods and services for attendees to consume and enjoy. The emphasis has been placed entirely on the product, namely the Sunday worship service. Churches then compete to produce more consumer-friendly and appealing services to attract and retain more "customers." When the church an individual attends is no longer meeting their needs, they go "church shopping" and find a church whose services are of greater quality. Now certainly there are times when someone may need to look for a new church, but what I'm pointing out is this consumeristic attitude that pillages a church for resources without giving back.

Many people have the same loyalty to their church that I have to Safeway. I like Safeway. I buy my groceries at Safeway. I'm loyal to

[125] See Robert N. Bellah et al. *Habits of the Heart: Individualism and Commitment in American Life* (Berkeley, CA: University of California Press, 1996).

Safeway. That is, unless something were to change. If they stopped giving out Airmiles or raised their prices, or reduced their staffing or stopped providing decent customer service, my loyalty would end and I would shop elsewhere. My loyalty is purely selfish. I'm loyal as long as I'm *getting* what I want, the way I want. If something better comes along, I'm gone. It's all about me and what I'm getting. This is (probably) an acceptable attitude when buying Cheerios and diapers. But a church isn't a store, it's a community.

In his book *Death by Suburb*, David Goetz concludes that most of us only know what he calls "transactional relationships."[126] I'll help you so that you'll help me. We maintain most of our relationships just as long as we personally benefit from them. We have no interest in real self-sacrificing, others-serving community. The gospel changes all that.

A PEOPLE, A NATION

In a packed and important section Paul tells Titus that "our great God and Savior Jesus Christ... gave himself for us to redeem us from all lawlessness and to purify for himself a people for his own possession who are zealous for good works."[127] According to this passage, at the cross, Jesus died for us to accomplish two things, the second of which is to create a people, a purified people, a people who belong to him and are passionate for doing good.

The Apostle Peter writes, "But you are a chosen race, a royal priesthood, a holy nation, a people for his own possession, that you may proclaim the excellencies of him who called you out of darkness into his marvelous light. Once you were not a people, but now you are God's

---

[126] David L. Goetz, *Death by Suburb: How to Keep the Suburbs from Killing Your Soul* (New York: HarperCollins, 2006), 149.
[127] Titus 2:13-14

people; once you had not received mercy, but now you have received mercy."[128] Pulling on the rich imagery of Exodus 19 and Deuteronomy 7, Peter describes Christians as a nation of priests and a people belonging to God. They are a new community, called out of darkness into light. There are no individual Christians who are not part of this people, this community.

But what type of people is this? We can experience connectedness and community on a basketball team or in a knitting club (I'm told). How is this new community formed? In the prologue of his gospel, John writes "But to all who did receive [Christ], who believed in his name, he gave the right to become children of God, who were born, not of blood nor of the will of the flesh nor of the will of man, but of God."[129] Paul picks up on this theme of adoption and adds that God "predestined us for *adoption as sons* through Jesus Christ, according to the purpose of his will."[130] When we hear the gospel and respond with repentance and faith we are adopted into a new family, we now belong to a new people of God. We no longer belong to self, but to God and to each other.

GOSPEL AND COMMUNITY

This new family is one that is radically centered around the gospel. It's the death and resurrection of Jesus that brings us into this new community and defines how we relate to each other. The story of the community is the story of the gospel. A church is not a weekly event or a program. It's not a building or a charitable organization. A church is a gospel-centered community, a people radically shaped by the grace of God in Christ.

---

[128] I Peter 2:9-10
[129] John 1:12-13
[130] Ephesians 1:5 emphasis mine; also Galatians 4:1-7; Romans 8:14-17

The gospel is not simply the entry point into the community but is the shaping force for how the community lives together. Paul urged the Ephesian church to "Let all bitterness and wrath and anger and clamor and slander be put away from you, along with all malice. Be kind to one another, tenderhearted, forgiving one another, *as God in Christ forgave you.*"[131] Do you see? Bitterness, anger, clamor, slander and malice must be put away in favor of kindness, tenderheartedness, and forgiveness. Why the trade? Because "God in Christ forgave you." The forgiveness of God, granted to us because of the substitutionary death of Christ, shapes the way the community relates to each other. Bitterness, malice and the like are unacceptable because that's not how God treated us, though we deserved that and much more. Instead we're called to mirror the kindness, tenderheartedness and forgiveness of God. As he has forgiven us our exorbitant debt, so to we are called to show forgiveness to others.

Jesus tells a parable of a man who has a ridiculously large and unpayable debt—billions of dollars by today's standards—which the king shockingly forgives. That newly forgiven servant turns around and physically attacks a man who owed him a fairly small amount—roughly $5000—completely unwilling to show any mercy. The king calls this unforgiving servant, and says, "should not you have had mercy on your fellow servant, as I had mercy on you?"[132] Jesus' point is obvious: as God has shown mercy and forgiveness to us, we need to show the mercy and forgiveness to those who have wronged us. The gospel shapes our behavior.

On another occasion Jesus said to his disciples, "A new commandment I give to you, that you love one another: *just as I have loved you*, you also are to love one another. By this all people will know that you are my

---

[131] Ephesians 4:31-32, emphasis mine.
[132] Matthew 18:33

disciples, if you have love for one another."[133] This new community is to be known for its radical, self-sacrificial love for others. So much so, that you will be able to identify true disciples of Jesus by their radical love. But again we see that it's the gospel that calls for this radical behavior: "just as I have loved you, you also are to love one another." We love one another as an outflow and response to Jesus' love for us. We love others as a community of people loved by Jesus.

Beyond love, our entire life together needs to be reflective of the gospel. Paul urges the Roman Christians to "welcome one another as Christ has welcomed you, for the glory of God."[134] Their harmonious and hospitable relationships are motivated by the sacrifice Christ made to welcome us into God's family for God's glory.

Then to the Corinthians, Paul urges that they should show generosity towards all those in need because of "the grace of our Lord Jesus Christ, that though he was rich, yet for your sake he became poor, so that you by his poverty might become rich."[135] Our generosity is simply a reflection of Jesus' generosity in sacrificing his comfort, power and security to be humbled to the lowest place in order to save sinners. We give because Jesus gave.

Do you see how the gospel must shape our community life together? As God the Father has generously given us every good and perfect gift, we are called to generously give to others. As God forgave us—his enemies—we too are called to forgive our enemies. As God showed patience and forbearance in our rebellion, so to we are called to be patient with others. As God sacrificed himself for us, we're called to sacrifice for others. The Christian community is called to live as a mirror of the gospel to each other, reflecting God's grace in community.

---

[133] John 13:34-35
[134] Romans 15:7
[135] 2 Corinthians 8:9

Because of the gospel we welcome strangers as friends, open our homes to others, we share our possessions with those in need and give to the poor, we love the unlovable, comfort the lonely, weep with the hurting and celebrate with the joyful. We share our lives with each other and make room for all.

EVERYONE'S A PRIEST

As Peter stated, the church is now "a royal priesthood."[136] This was always God's heart. When he redeemed Israel out of slavery in Egypt and entered covenant with them, his desire was for them to be "a kingdom of priests and a holy nation."[137] They were to be a nation where everyone was a priest; everyone served God and performed ministry.

In a gospel-shaped community, every person is a minister of the gospel. Many of us think of ministry as the job of paid pastors and church staff, the trained few, but that's not right. Paul urges that the job of church leaders isn't to do ministry but "to equip the saints for the work of ministry, for building up the body of Christ."[138] Paul pictures the whole church ministering to the whole church until the whole church attains maturity in Christ. This ministry happens as we apply the gospel to each other's hearts, reminding one another of the truth of the gospel, identifying identity distortions and disbelief in our lives, and spurring each other on to gospel growth.

We no longer live simply for ourselves, but for the good and growth of our new family. We share our lives with others, opening our hearts and homes. We love, serve, nurture and care for each other. We provide for each other's needs. We live generously with others, recognizing that

---

[136] I Peter 2:9
[137] Exodus 19:6
[138] Ephesians 4:12

all that we have is simply entrusted to us by God to be used for gospel ministry.

As a true community we are open, vulnerable and honest with each other. Because our life together is shaped by the gospel, we don't have to perform and pretend in order to impress others. What binds us together is our common brokenness, confession of sin and need for God's grace. Repentance, forgiveness and grace are at the very centre of our life to-gether. With the gospel as our example and motivation, we welcome sinners and speak words of grace instead of condemnation. We bring hope, mercy and gospel transformation to bear on all situations. We truly want the gospel to define all our relationships and be at the center of who we are as a community.

This understanding should radically alter the way we view church. Many people have a distorted view of what a church is. You can see it in the language we use. A church is not a charitable organization or an institution ("I donated it to the church"). A church is not a building with a steeple and a cross ("we're meeting at the church"). A church is not a Sunday program or ministry that you can attend ("hurry up, we're going to be late for church"). In the Bible, the word church never refers to an institution, a building or an event. Instead a church is a people changed by Jesus, a people who define themselves by the gospel.

We don't stop being the church when the music ends. Theologians talk about the church *gathered* and the church *scattered*, recognizing that we are just as much the church when we are at home and work as we are when we are all in the same room together. A church gathers and scatters but it doesn't end.

Church is something we are, and something we pursue together. In a local church, we covenant together to *be* the church. We are promis-ing each other, the leadership and God that we will pursue living out gospel-centered community together. It won't be easy, that much is certain. Everything within our broken, selfish soul will fight community and embrace consumerism. But as God's people, his adopted children, we are called to pursue *being* the family of God, sharing our lives with one another, and allowing the gospel to shape our identity and life as a community.

Our gospel-shaped identity simply won't allow us to become consumeristic Christians, pillaging other Christians for resources without community or service. In the gospel we realize that we aren't simply saved as individuals alone on an island. We're saved into a family, a people, a community that is radically shaped by the gospel. Because of the story of God, we cannot live as lone rangers, but we're called to live out God's story in community with others, as the bought and saved family of God.

chapter 9

the gospel restores true worship

"Our hearts are restless until they rest in you" – Augustine

I recall a day when the TV channel TLC stood for The Learning Channel. I'm not sure when, but at some point they abandoned learning and seem to now be pursuing the strange and unusual. Hoarders, gypsy weddings, families with enough kids to start two baseball teams, a guy with three too many wives—this channel has all the weird you can handle. But a show that caught my eye recently is *Extreme Couponing*, a show about people who are obsessive about finding coupons and deals to the point where they get hundreds of dollars in groceries for just a few dollars and then hoard away their products in a massive stockpile in their basement.

Treasure Phillips is a 45 year old small business owner in Groton, Connecticut. "I love my stockpile. I love it" she says. "If my stockpile were to just somehow disappear, having it gone would be like taking away a part of our family." You can see a glimpse of panic on her face as she considers life without her stockpile of over 6,000 products, worth over $35,000. The camera shows her dusting her shelves upon shelves of products, with more mustard and fabric softener than the two-baseball team family could use in a lifetime. She says, "I would liken my couponing to training as an Olympic athlete always, always thinking about training. I'm always, always thinking about coupons."

Some people featured on the show are motivated by saving money or helping others, like the one couple who got several hundred dollars of products for a only a few dollars and then gave it all away to a local homeless shelter. But with Treasure and others, her couponing is not a practical necessity but is a longing of the heart. She loves her stock-pile. She can't think about living without it. She's always, always thinking about coupons and how to get more products for free. Enough is never enough. This is not shopping. This is worship.

CONTINUOUS OUTPOURING

When you think of worship, you might naturally think of singing in a church building or bowing in a temple. While those activities could be, worship is so much bigger than that. In his excellent book *Unceasing Worship*, Harold Best defines it this way, "Worship is the continuous outpouring of all that I am, all that I do and all that I can ever become in light of a chosen or choosing god."[139] By continuous he means re-lentless, being the opposite of periodic or sporadic. By outpouring he implies "lavishness and generosity: when I pour something, I give it up; I let it go."[140] He goes on to say, "because God is the Continuous Outpourer, we bear his image as continuous outpourers... we were cre-ated continuously outpouring."[141] He doesn't say that we were "made to

---

[139] Harold M. Best, *Unceasing Worship: Biblical Perspectives on Worship and the Arts* (Downers Grove, IL: Intervarsity Press, 2003), 18.
[140] Ibid., 19.
[141] Ibid., 23.

worship" as that would suggest that worship is something we should, but don't always do. That's not quite right. Worship is not something you can ever cease doing. We weren't made to worship, we were made worshipping. We are always worshipping. All of us. There is no one who is not a worshipper.

But what of the fall? Did sin ruin our continuous outpouring? Best explains,

> The fall did not signal the end of worship or continuous outpouring. Something deeper happened, far down in our being, whereby our entirety was inverted and turned to ruin. We chose to believe a lie, spoken by one with whom truth is impossible but who skillfully dresses falsehood in light. We took to this reversed light and were immediately lost and undone. Our outpouring was falsified. But it continued, with one telling difference: we exchanged gods.... In short, we became idolaters, for the worship of anything but God alone is idolatry.[142]

We are all always worshipping. We were made worshipping. The fall didn't put an end to our worship, it simply redirected it. The worship that rightly belongs to the Creator is poured out for his creation. We've tragically exchanged gods.

A FACTORY OF IDOLS

An idol is not necessarily a statue that we bow down to—it rarely is. It's important to note that the wooden and stone statues of ancient times were merely the physical representations of the idols that took up residence in their hearts. Idolatry starts in the heart with a change of

---

[142] Ibid., 25-26.

allegiance, a redirecting of worship. Bowing in front of a statue was simply the final step in a long journey of idolatry. We may never lay prostrate before our idols, but that doesn't make them any less idolatrous.

Additionally, an idol need not even be an evil thing—often it is a good thing. An idol is anything that takes God's place as our supreme treasure, joy and delight, the thing we look to for meaning, significance and purpose. Greg Beale, building off of Luther's definition says that an idol is "whatever your heart clings to or relies on for *ultimate security*."[143] Tim Keller says it this way: "[an idol] is anything more important to you than God, anything that absorbs your heart and imagination more than God, anything you seek to give you what only God can give."[144] You can see that anything can be an idol. Any failure to live with God as your heart's supreme joy, delight and security is idolatry. As broken humans, created as worshippers, we are continually finding new and creative ways to commit idolatry. John Calvin is famously quoted as saying "the human heart is a factory of idols." In our broken state, we are inclined to turn anything and everything into a god.

In Ezekiel 14, the elders of Israel would have been shocked when they were accused by God of committing idolatry. Where were their idols? What statues did they bow down to? God says of them, "these men have taken their idols into their hearts."[145] While in many parts of the world people still bow down before statues, idolatry in the human heart is global. Paul warns the Colossian church of the danger of covetousness, "which is idolatry."[146] When your heart is dissatisfied with God and seeks delight in having your neighbor's possessions, you are

[143] G.K. Beale, *We Become What We Worship: A Biblical Theology of Idolatry* (Downers Grove, IL: Intervarsity Press, 2008), 17.
[144] Timothy Keller, *Counterfeit Gods: The Empty Promises of Money, Sex, and Power, and the Only Hope That Matters* (New York: Dutton, 2009), xvii.
[145] Ezekiel 14:3
[146] Colossians 3:5

committing idolatry in your heart. Money so easily and quickly can become the object of our affection and outpouring. A.W. Tozer warns of slavery to the "tyranny of things."[147] Without active resistance, the pursuit of possessions can easily possess us. Likewise Paul warned the Philippians of certain "enemies of the cross" who are idolaters: "their god is their belly, and they glory in their shame, with minds set on earthly things."[148] In this form of idolatry, these men worshipped indulgence and consumption and had made a god of their belly. All of life is lived as a continuous outpouring towards their own consumption.

We could make an endless list of idols. We commit idolatry when we pour ourselves out on the altar of our career and look to success, power and position as our ultimate security and joy.

Others find ultimate meaning in sex, believing that either enough quality or quantity or variety of sexual experiences will bring them the true satisfaction and significance that they crave.

Many single people make an idol out of marriage, believing that if only they had a spouse, they would be content. But Jerry Maguire got it all wrong when he overdramatically proclaimed "you complete me." Looking to a spouse—future or present—for ultimate meaning, joy and security is an act of idolatry and a shortcut to disappointment. A spouse can be a wonderful gift, but will always make a terrible god.

You could add power, influence, leisure and work as common things which are elevated from good gifts to be enjoyed, to idols that we sacrifice our entire being for. We are constantly finding new and creative ways to *not* worship God.

Factory of idols, indeed.

---

[147] Tozer, *The Pursuit of God*, 19.
[148] Philippians 3:19

SCRAPED KNEES

Imagine I'm out in the yard where my daughter Eva is playing. Now imagine that her clumsy two-year-old feet trip and she tumbles to the ground. With eyes full of tears and sobs that melt a daddy's heart, she picks herself up off the ground and runs past me and down the driveway, across the yard to the neighbours house! Instead of running to her daddy and looking for comfort, care and affection from me, she runs past me to the neighbour. Our neighbours are nice people. I have no complaints about them. But *I'm* Eva's dad! She should run *to* me. I care for her, love her, will protect her and make everything better. I'm her co-creator!

In this analogy, Eva is an idolater. She has exchanged her relationship with her father for one with a stranger. She has taken a good thing (a nice neighbour) and made it into an ultimate thing (replacement parent/rescuer). My heart longs for my baby girl to find her protection and safety in my arms, and to see her run anywhere else would be heartbreaking.[149] In idolatrous behaviour, we run past our Father and Maker and find our consolation, joy, rescue and love somewhere else. As I think about my daughter running past me into the arms of a stranger I can begin to imagine how hurtful and offensive idolatry is to God.

The first of the Ten Commandments is "you shall have no other gods before me."[150] It's not that God is a cranky and selfish god. My desire to be Eva's sole rescuer and to not share her with the neighbour doesn't make me cranky and selfish, but a good dad. I won't trust her into the arms of those who would abuse her. It's God's love for us that demands that he be our only god.

---

[149] I know what you're thinking, and no, I have no ability to fathom my daughter getting married someday.
[150] Exodus 20:3

THE GOSPEL AND TRUE WORSHIP

The gospel sets us free from our idolatry and refocuses our worship back to where it belongs. In Christ, we finally are able to truly worship. Augustine started his *Confessions* by saying, "You awaken us to delight in Your praise, for You made us for Yourself and our hearts are restless until they rest in you."[151] At the fall we exchanged the glory of the immortal God for images and we worshipped and served the creature rather than the Creator.[152] With the gospel, this exchange is reversed. We are able to repent of our idolatry and find our ultimate joy, delight and security in God.

Our hearts long to admire beauty. In the face of God we see ultimate and true beauty. Our hearts desire to worship a champion. We celebrate our athletic heroes like gods. Jesus is the greatest victor having once-for-all conquered Satan, sin and death at the cross. Our hearts long for love and acceptance. The truest sacrificial love is seen in Christ giving himself up for his enemies. We desire true lasting joy and delight, and will mortgage our life believing the false promises of wealth and possessions. But God alone is the true desire of our heart, the only one that will satisfy us. We crave purpose and significance and are willing sacrifice our children on the altar of our career just to be recognized as important. Yet, our real significance comes in identifying in the gospel story, that we are made in the image of God, broken sinners, redeemed by God's grace, called to live and work for his purposes in the world. Our lives have eternal significance as we work for a Kingdom that will not end and a King that will not die.

---

[151] St. Augustine, *The Confessions of St. Augustine*, (New Kensington, PA: Whitaker House, 1996), 11.
[152] Romans 1:23, 25

COMMANDED TO DELIGHT?

Somewhere along the way it became popular to equate Christian maturity to a sober fulfillment of duty. Godliness was measured in seriousness. The attitude seems to be that the Christian life is meant to be painful and serious now and joyful in eternity. It's a short term pain for long term gain sort of deal. This is so wrong.

The Scriptures never portray the appropriate response to God as dispassionate, dutiful, sober obedience. On the contrary! We are instructed to delight in the law,[153] to delight in doing God's will,[154] and to delight in God himself.[155] We are commanded to rejoice in the Lord in all circumstances, again Paul says, rejoice![156] Our entire lives are to be one of worshipful response.[157] Jesus instructs us that obedience to his words leads to maximum joy.[158] What kind of giver does God love? Not a reluctant one or one under compulsion, for "God loves a *cheerful* giver."[159] Over and over again we are commanded—yes commanded!—to delight in God. It's wrong to think that the world offers pleasure, while God calls us to duty.

The truth is that the world offers fake pleasure, while God offers real pleasure. "In your presence there is fullness of joy; at your right hand are pleasures forevermore."[160] God alone satisfies the longing of our hearts. God alone offers true joy. All other promises of joy will fail us and let us down: "Whom have I in heaven but you? And there is nothing on earth that I desire besides you. My flesh and my heart may fail, but

---

[153] Psalm 1:2
[154] Psalm 40:8
[155] Psalm 37:4
[156] Philippians 4:4; also Philippians 3:1
[157] Romans 12:1
[158] John 15:11
[159] 2 Corinthians 9:7
[160] Psalm 16:11

God is the strength of my heart and my portion forever."[161] Our bodies and hearts *will* fail us. So will our cars, our homes, our family, our work and our hobbies. God alone will truly fulfill our desires.

As we encounter God's truth, revealed in Jesus, we cannot remain the same. Truth leads us to a joyful, spiritual, passionate, worshipful, God-magnifying, satisfying, emotional, active response. We don't just understand truth, but we *feel* it. Worship is a response to God that engages the mind and the heart.[162] This is such a theme in the New Testament, that to grow in maturity is not to grow in information, but to grow in passion and love for Jesus. As the gospel shapes us, we live more and more for God's glory and joyful delight in him.

John Piper puts it this way, "God is most glorified in us, when we are most satisfied in Him."[163] The purpose of life is to glorify God, and the best way we can possibly do that is for us to find our satisfaction in God, and thus show him to be supremely satisfying over all else. Well before Piper, C.S. Lewis wrote, "the Scotch Catechism says that man's chief end is 'to glorify God and enjoy Him forever'. But we shall then know that these are the same thing. Fully to enjoy is to glorify. In commanding us to glorify Him, God is inviting us to enjoy Him."[164] We don't worship through painful and joyless duty. That doesn't honor God. It actually diminishes his glory. What brings God maximum glory in our lives is when we worship by finding our delight, joy and satisfaction in him. In so doing we display him as the supreme treasure of the universe and the One that our hearts have always longed for.

Lewis, one last time:

If there lurks in most modern minds the notion that to desire our

---

[161] Psalm 73:25-26
[162] John 4:23
[163] John Piper, *Desiring God: Meditations of a Christian Hedonist* (Colorado Springs, CO: Multnomah Books, 2003), 288.
[164] C.S. Lewis, *Reflections on the Psalms* (London: Fontana Books, 1958), 82.

own good and earnestly to hope for the enjoyment of it is a bad thing, I submit that this notion has crept in from Kant and the Stoics and is no part of the Christian faith. Indeed, if we consider the unblushing promises of reward and the staggering nature of the rewards promised in the Gospels, it would seem that Our Lord finds our desires not too strong, but too weak. We are half-hearted creatures, fooling about with drink and sex and ambition when infinite joy is offered us, like an ignorant child who wants to go on making mud pies in a slum because he cannot imagine what is meant by the offer of a holiday at the sea. We are far too easily pleased.[165]

WORSHIP YOUR WAY OUT OF SIN

It was worship that got us into this mess of sin, exchanging the glory of the Creator for images of created things. And being freed by Jesus, it is by worship that we live free from sin.

Every Christian fails. We live in this awkward between-the-ages time when salvation is both here and coming. We've tasted redemption and long for the final redemption to come. Until then, though we are no longer enslaved to sin, we still fall into it. We still fail.

Our default response is hard work. We scold ourselves and then demand more: "you're better than that. Smarten up!" We create accountability groups that demand honesty about our behaviours because we fear what people think more than we fear God. We pick ourselves up and try again to overcome through another dose of white-knuckled perseverance. This effort-driven sanctification just doesn't work. Shame, duty, effort and sober discipline can temporarily change our behaviours

---

[165] C.S. Lewis, *The Weight of Glory: And Other Addresses* (New York: HarperCollins, 1980), 26.

but it will never change our hearts. Our sin problem is a worship problem.

Thomas Chalmers, the 19th century Scottish pastor, preached a famous sermon called "The Expulsive Power of a New Affection." He argued that even the strongest resolve will never be enough to overcome a sinful desire. You simply cannot will your way out of sin.[166] That sinful desire cannot be replaced with a void, but must be replaced with a new desire, a new affection. This new affection expels the old affection.

The gospel sets us free from our old desires and gives us new desires. Our old desires and new desires are in competition with each other.[167] The answer isn't to kill all desires, but to so pursue Jesus, to so delight in God's glory, to so enjoy the gospel that the old desires are replaced and expelled by the new desires for God. How do we overcome our sin and failures? With more worship.

LIVING LIFE AS WORSHIPFUL RESPONSE

So when we think of Christian worship, it is of an entirely different order than the worship mandated by other religions. Christianity has no temple or holy places. There are no sacrifices offered on an altar. There is no enshrined burial site of its founder, as the tomb is empty. When a Samaritan woman wants to engage Jesus in the age-old argument about what location is the only correct one for worship—Jerusalem or Mt. Gerizim—Jesus tells her that both answers are wrong. Neither location is right. He said, "But the hour is coming, and is now here, when the true worshipers will worship the Father in spirit and truth, for the Father is seeking such people to worship him. God is spirit, and those who

---

[166] In contrast to Christian band DCTalk who sang "will power/ the power to will away temptation."
[167] Galatians 5:17

worship him must worship in spirit and truth."[168] In other words, true worship is God-centred; it is worship of the Father. True worship is spiritual, not just physical. So the location is irrelevant. Christianity has no holy places or temples because Christian worship is a spiritual act rather than a strictly physical one. "Do you not know that you are God's temple and that God's Spirit dwells in you?"[169] Instead of dwelling in a physical structure, God dwells within us. Finally, worship flows out of truth. Worshipping in error isn't true worship. True worship is an active response to the gospel story. We encounter God's truth in the gospel and respond with a life of spiritual worship for his glory.

We should worship as the gathered church through singing, prayer, giving of our finances, the preaching of God's word and the right observance of baptism and the Lord's Supper. We gather to worship in unison, together pouring ourselves out for God's glory. But we also can worship in a thousand others ways. We can worship as we serve others in need, listen to good music, create a short film, go for a hike in the mountains, read a good book, work and create, raise children or weed the garden. Any of these activities and many more *can* be worship of God if they are done as an outpouring for God's glory, as a way of delighting in his supreme worth.

You can plant flowers in such a way that you delight in flowers as an end to themselves. And there is a way that you can plant flowers as a way to delight in God and display his glory. The difference isn't in the flowers but in your heart.

Paul urges the church in Rome, "I appeal to you therefore, brothers, by the mercies of God, to present your bodies as a living sacrifice, holy and acceptable to God, which is your spiritual worship."[170] For the

---

[168] John 4:23–24
[169] I Corinthians 3:16; also 6:19
[170] Romans 12:1

Christian, worship is not a physical act done in a particular place. We don't offer a sacrifice on an altar or in a temple. Christian worship is a perpetual sacrificing of myself; a continual outpouring of all that I am, all that I do and all that I can ever become for the glory of God and for my joy. True worship is a joyful, passionate, God-glorifying life lived in response to the gospel. The story of God moves us to respond with a life of continuous outpouring for God's glory.

Chapter 10

the gospel sends us on mission

"Go and make disciples" - Jesus

We all want a life of purpose and significance. We want to make a difference with our lives and leave behind a legacy. We want our life to really matter. You see this in the overachieving grade 12 academic superstar kids who are determined to get straight A's, get into the best university, get the best job and really make something of themselves. The belief is that if they work hard enough their life can really matter. But we also see this in the underachieving kids (and adults) playing Xbox every waking moment. Every guy has this innate desire to be part of a team, be given a crucial life or death mission, make a difference and save lives. If you can't live a life that really matters, might as well pretend, right? A whole generation of man-boys were never trained to be men and now live out their God-given calling to live with purpose and mission by playing Halo. God has so much more for us. He is calling us to join the team, get on the mission, make a difference for eternity and see lives be changed by the gospel.

MISSIONARY GOD, MISSIONARY PEOPLE

The story of God is told in four acts: creation, fall, redemption, restoration. But it didn't have to be this way. The story could have gone creation, fall, judgment. The end. It could have ended with our sin and rebellion, but instead God embarked on a mission to glorify his name by redeeming a people for his own possession. God is a missionary, who is a sender by nature. In the Old Testament, God sent Israel to the nations, to draw people to Jerusalem to worship him. Israel was called to be "a kingdom of priests and a holy nation"[171] with the goal that all the nations would flow to Jerusalem, to worship God at his temple,[172] which was to be called "a house of prayer *for all peoples*."[173] This is the centripetal mission of Israel, to live in covenant with God in such a way that the nations would be drawn to Jerusalem to worship him there.

When they fail in this mission and break covenant, God sends his prophets to call his people to repentance and covenant renewal. The prophets begin to envision a day when God will send a second but greater prophet like Moses,[174] a second but greater (and eternal) king like David,[175] and a righteous but suffering servant who will die for the people.[176] God, through the prophet Malachi says "I will send my messenger and he will prepare the way before me" and "I will send you Elijah the prophet before the great and awesome day of the LORD comes."[177]

As we arrive in the New Testament, we see that God, the great Sender, has now sent his Son. *Forty times* in the gospel of John does Jesus claim that he was sent from the Father. Forty times in just twenty one chapters! Jesus says, "For I have come down from heaven, not to do my

---

[171] Exodus 19:6
[172] Isaiah 2:2-3; Jeremiah 3:15-18;
[173] Isaiah 56:7, emphasis mine.
[174] Deuteronomy 18:15-18; 34:10-12
[175] 2 Samuel 7:12-16; Isaiah 9:6-7; 11:1-9;
[176] Isaiah 42:1-9; 49:1-6; 50:4-9; 52:13-53:12
[177] Malachi 3:1 & 4:5

own will but the will of him who sent me"[178] and "I have not spoken on my own authority, but the Father who sent me has himself given me a commandment—what to say and what to speak."[179] Jesus repeatedly emphasized that he was not there on his own authority, or to fulfill his own mission, but was sent by the Father. The Sending God has sent his own Son.

And then in two very crucial moments in John's gospel, Jesus turns and tells his disciples that they too have been sent on mission. He says "As the Father has sent me, even so I am sending you."[180] To be a disciple of Jesus is to be sent on mission by Jesus. This is not the calling of some disciples, but is the mandate for all Christians. Just before his ascension, Jesus tells his disciples, "you will receive power when the Holy Spirit has come upon you, and you will be my witnesses in Jerusalem and in all Judea and Samaria, and to the end of the earth."[181] Here we see a great reversal in the mission of God. The mission is no longer a centripetal mission (drawing the nations in), but is now a centrifugal mission (sending his people out to the nations).[182]

I find this truly amazing and humbling. God certainly doesn't need us. There is no lack in God that I somehow fulfill. God doesn't *need* teammates. I'm more liability than asset in the task of redeeming the world. "Together we're better" doesn't apply to an all-powerful, all-sufficient, sovereign God. Paul says that

> [God] through Christ reconciled us to himself and gave us the ministry of reconciliation; that is, in Christ God was reconciling the world to himself, not counting their trespasses against them, and

---

[178] John 6:38
[179] John 12:49
[180] John 20:21; see also 17:18
[181] Acts 1:8
[182] I'm not sure if this is included in one of his many books, but this observation came from a lecture with the brilliant Ed Stetzer at Re:Train in November 2010.

entrusting to us the message of reconciliation. Therefore, we are ambassadors for Christ, God making his appeal through us.[183] God saves us, makes us into a new creation, and then sends us to bring his message of reconciliation to our world. We are his ambassadors. We are sent as his official representatives on earth. In the great mission of God, his sovereign plan of reconciling the world to himself through the cross, God has chosen to make his appeal through us. Amazing! Ed Stetzer summarizes,

> The sending God sent the Son. We join him in his mission of seeking and saving the lost. Then we become God's sent people to proclaim the message of repentance and forgiveness in the power of the Holy Spirit both locally and worldwide to all people groups.[184]

He welcomes us into the unfolding story of the advance of the gospel. We aren't sideline observers, but are active participants in his mission. The gospel saves us and sends us.

DISCIPLE-MAKING DISCIPLES

What then is the mission? The mission of the church—given by Jesus—is to make disciples: "Go therefore and make disciples of all nations, baptizing them in the name of the Father and of the Son and of the Holy Spirit, teaching them to observe all that I have commanded you."[185] Part of that disciple-making process is to teach those disciples to obey Jesus' commands, which of course includes the command in the prior verse to go and make disciples! A true and faithful disciple of Jesus is one who makes disciples who make disciples.

---

[183] 2 Corinthians 5:18-20
[184] Ed Stetzer, *Planting Missional Churches* (Nashville, TN: B&H Publishing, 2006), 43.
[185] Matthew 28:19-20

Typically we have read this commission of Jesus as a command to send money and missionaries to other parts of the world. That may be part of it, but we need to see this commission is not primarily about mission somewhere else. As Marshall and Payne say, "it's a commission that makes disciple-making the normal agenda and priority of every church and every Christian disciple."[186] I'm not saying that we shouldn't send missionaries overseas. We need to. Our church is in the process of sending Simon—a guy who grew up in our church—to Northern Kenya to bring the gospel of Jesus to unreached nomadic tribes. This is a very important work. We need to be working to see the gospel proclaimed and churches planted among unreached people groups. But we also need to widen our understanding of mission and ministry to include what Jesus is calling us to do at home and not just what he's calling us to do abroad.

One of the challenges to mission is that most Christians have an overly-institutionalized understanding of mission and ministry. When we think of mission, we think of missionaries travelling to Africa to preach the gospel to those who have not yet heard about Jesus. And when we think of doing ministry we think of serving in the programs in the church. The real work of mission and ministry is not programs but people. We're on mission with Jesus when we are applying the gospel to people's hearts, helping them to become fully-formed disciples of Jesus.

In his prayer for the Colossians, Paul says "Of this you have heard before in the word of the truth, the gospel, which has come to you, as indeed in the whole world it is bearing fruit and growing—as it also does among you, since the day you heard it and understood the grace of God in truth."[187] We pray and work to see the word of the truth, the gospel,

---

[186] Colin Marshall and Tony Payne, *The Trellis and the Vine: The Ministry Mind-Shift that Changes Everything* (Kingsford, AU: Matthias Media, 2009), 13.

[187] Colossians 1:5-6

take root, grow and bear fruit in the hearts of individuals. We work to see the *gospel* growing in people. Christian growth *is* gospel growth.

How do we do gospel ministry? By proclaiming the gospel and applying it to the lives of those God is calling you to minister to. It may be the people in your community group, it may be friends from within the church, it may be co-workers or neighbours, but God is calling you to be making disciples.

We make disciples by reminding people of the gospel. The reason why we distort our identity is because we exchange the truth of the gospel for the lies of Satan, forgetting who we are in Christ. The reason why we fall into idolatry is because we disbelieve the sufficiency and delight of God and we exchange true worship of God for worship of created things which will never satisfy.

The reason why we fall into any sin is because in that moment we fail to believe the gospel. There is something about God's character and the gospel message which we fail to believe when we act sinfully. We don't trust his supremacy or his goodness, and so we live with anxiety and worry. We don't believe he is perfect justice and righteousness, so we take revenge and lash out against our enemies. We don't believe that Jesus fully covered our debt of sin, and so we labour religiously to put God in our debt. We don't believe that God is our all-satisfying treasure and so we seek pleasure in money, success and sex instead. We don't believe that we were truly enemies of God deserving hell and completely undeserving of God's kindness, and so we treat our enemies with contempt instead of grace. We don't believe that we truly did not deserve for Christ to love us and to give himself up for us, and so we fail to love and sacrifice for our spouse when they don't deserve it. In every sin, in every failure, we fail to believe the gospel.

We fight sin and we make disciples by teaching, proclaiming and reminding people of the gospel. We so easily forget that our identity is

founded in Christ's success and not ours. We so easily abandon community for consumerism and worship for idolatry. In community, we need
to be constantly reminding each other of the gospel, reminding each
other of our Hero. We use right beliefs to combat each other's wrong
beliefs. We help each other to remember the Story of God and to find
our place in it.

OUT OF THE BUBBLE

One of the biggest obstacles to faithful mission is that many Christians
live in a bubble. We've created this evangelical subculture to insulate
ourselves from the big, bad world. We have Christian stores, Christian
books, Christian music, Christian concerts, Christian radio stations,
Christian clothing companies, Christian TV channels, Christian greet-
ing cards, Christian retirement complexes, Christian cruise ships and
vacations, Christian coffee shops, Christian dating services, Christian
schools, Christian businesses, Christian "art"[188] and Christian trinkets of
every kind. We even have Christian breath mints. How is that possible?
Could someone explain to me how a breath mint becomes a Christian?

Some of these things may have some value, but some Christians
have worked really hard to create an entire Christian subculture so that
they can entirely avoid coming into contact with people who don't know
Jesus. They surround themselves exclusively with people who are exactly like them. Some Christian groups actually live on a colony physically separated from the world, while other Christians live on a *relational*
colony, having isolated themselves from the very culture they are called
to reach with the gospel. They may not sport neck-beards or churn their
own butter, but they are living as if on a colony just the same.

---

[188] ie. kitch.

Jesus actually prayed for his disciples, saying

> I do not ask that you take them out of the world, but that you
> keep them from the evil one. They are not of the world, just as
> I am not of the world. Sanctify them in the truth; your word is
> truth. As you sent me into the world, so I have sent them into the
> world.[189]

Jesus specifically prays that we wouldn't be taken out of the world.
Protection is not found in physical or relational separation from non-
Christians, but is found in being tethered to the truth, God's word. Jesus
prays that as he sends us, we'd be protected, not by being separated, but
by staying in the truth.

Our perfect example of this is Jesus himself. Missional living is simply living like Jesus. Jesus was a missionary, who came and lived right in
the midst of a sinful and rebellious world, surrounded by people who
were separated from God. But, by the power of the Holy Spirit, he lived
a faithful, godly life in the midst of that culture, always pointing people
to the gospel of grace. He neither hid from sinful culture, nor was he
influenced by sinful culture. His entire life was lived as a sent missionary:
knowing and living in culture, loving people deeply and pointing everyone to the gospel. Living on mission is to live like Jesus.

GOSPEL INTENTIONALITY

You are not where you are by accident. The Bible teaches that in his
sovereignty God has ordained our days and places.[190] God has placed
you in the job, home, family and relationships that you find yourself in.
Combine that truth with the truth that we are all sent as missionaries,
representing Jesus to our world, and this means that we need to live with

---

[189] John 17:15-18
[190] Acts 17:26

a *gospel intentionality*, discerning the unique relationships and opportunities that God has given each of us, and then using those situations to build deeper relationships, love and serve others, and to share Jesus. While many people float through life without purpose, faithful Christians are intentional about mission and their missional call affects how and where they live, eat, play, learn, work and rest. All of life is mission.

But, one of the primary reasons that Christians are not faithful missionaries in their God-ordained situations is that they simply do not love non-Christians. Unlike Jesus, we do not love sinners. For many Christians, the only non-Christians they'll build a meaningful relationship with are those who are potential Christians. In other words, "I'll like you as long as I can change you to be more like me". We need to repent of our failure to genuinely love non-Christians as Jesus does and pray that God gives us a love for sinners as he unconditionally loves them.

We need to let the gospel story shape our view of other people. Your neighbour is an image-bearer of God, created with purpose and intentionality. Though they are broken, sinful and rebellious, they are still loved by God. You are called to reflect the gospel to them. As God loved you, forgave you, generously gave grace and mercy to you, showed you hospitality and immeasurable kindness, so to you need to give the same to your neighbour, even if they make you to be their enemy as you did to God.

When we live a non-religious life, with the gospel as our identity, sharing our lives with others in community and living all of life as worship to God, we will naturally be faithful missionaries. The truly gospel-shaped life is remarkable, attractive and compelling.

My friend Sandy will hire an esthetician for the day and invite her friends and neighbours over to get treated. She uses this as an opportunity to spend the whole day talking and sharing Jesus with everyone. Making disciples of Jesus while getting your nails done.

My wife goes to her massage therapist to share Jesus with her. What else are you going to talk about for 45 minutes, the weather? Sometimes she just goes more for the mission than the massage.

When I was fourteen, I decided to change from the Christian school I was attending to the local public high school. Now that I had the gospel, I felt I couldn't stay in a private school, but must take the message of Jesus to where it was needed most.

I served on the strata council in my condo building, not because I like building management and meetings—I hate both—but because it was a way for me to meet and serve my neighbours. God had placed us in that building, and the mission of Jesus meant getting out, serving others and sharing Jesus with my building.

A friend of ours chose to put her kids into a non-Christian preschool so that she could share Jesus with the other moms. After months of good conversations and discussion about Jesus she took about a dozen of them through a study of Tim Keller's book *The Reason for God*, introducing them to the gospel.

When my mother-in-law was a palliative care nurse she would share the gospel with dying patients and offer to pray with them, giving them nurture and care in their last days.

Marie Ens and her husband Norm were missionaries with the Christians & Missionary Alliance for 44 years. At age 66, after serving overseas for all those years, and faithfully caring for Norm until his death, now at the age of retirement, it would make sense for Marie to settle down back in Canada as a widow and retired missionary. Instead, Marie moved back to Cambodia, living off her pension, and in 2003 started Place of Rescue, an orphanage that is now home to 196 orphans, and 23 destitute elderly women. Place of Rescue II is home to another 100 orphans and plans are in place for a third Place of Rescue. For most people retirement is a time for indulgence and relaxation. For Marie, retirement means saving lives and making a difference for hundreds in the name of Jesus. Nearing 80, Marie still lives on mission with Jesus. While so many lives end with a whimper, Marie is finishing with a God-glorifying roar.[191]

There are endless other ways to live on mission with Jesus. Join a sports team or community club, organize a block party, have your neighbours or co-workers over for dinner. Be intentional and think mission when you get your haircut or go to the dentist. All of life is mission. Where is God calling you? To whom has God sent you on mission?

---

[191] Visit www.placeofrescue.com to learn more.

join the story

As a pastor I've performed many, many funerals. I find funerals fascinating. People's worldview will radically shape the way they deal with death. I've stood at the head of an open grave while family members wept inconsolably while a heavy despair filled the air. And I've stood in the same spot while a family reminisced with joy and broke into song in the middle of the cemetery. But what I find most fascinating at funerals is the tribute. How do you sum up 80 years in 10 minutes? I've often sat through a tribute of a person I had never met, and wondered, is that it? Is there nothing else to say about them? Do memories about playing darts, cheering on the Canucks and camping at the lake really capture a life?

I'm afraid many people miss out on life. They work so hard to convince themselves and those around them that they have everything under control. They're the hero that saves the day. We write our own stories. We do it our own way. We dance to the beat of our own drum. We waste our lives.

The gospel story invites us in. God is inviting us to find our identity in his story, not our own. He calls us to find our part in the grand story of the world, a story of creation, fall, redemption and restoration, a story of a good and gracious God pursuing and saving his people. Let the story of God fully shape your life and define your mission. Live with Jesus as the Hero. Let the gospel be your identity. Let your life's story be a reflection of the story of God. Now that's an unwasted life.